Bioethics in a
Liberal Society

Bioethics in a Liberal Society

MAX CHARLESWORTH

Emeritus Professor of Philosophy,
Deakin University

CAMBRIDGE
UNIVERSITY PRESS

Published by the Press Syndicate of the University of Cambridge.
The Pitt Building, Trumpington Street, Cambridge CB2 1RP, UK
40 West 20th Street, New York, NY 10011-4211, USA
10 Stamford Road, Oakleigh, Melbourne 3166, Australia

© Cambridge University Press 1993
First published 1993

Printed in Hong Kong by Colorcraft

National Library of Australia cataloguing in publication data
Charlesworth, Max, 1925–
Bioethics in a liberal society.
Includes index.
ISBN 0 521 44503 5.
ISBN 0 521 44952 9 (pbk.).
1. Bioethics. 2. Medical ethics. 3. Biotechnology — Moral and
ethical aspects. I. Title.
174.9574

Library of Congress cataloguing in publication data
Charlesworth, M. J. (Maxwell John), 1925–
Bioethics in a liberal society/Max Charlesworth.
Includes bibliographical references and index.
ISBN 0-521-44503-5 (hardback). — ISBN 0-521-44952-9 (pbk.)
1. Medical ethics. I. Title.
[DNLM: 1. Bioethics. 2. Ethics, Medical. W 50 C477d 1993]
R724.C455 1993
174'.2–dc20
DNLM/DLC
for Library of Congress   93-18160
                                                              CIP

A catalogue record for this book is available from the British Library.
ISBN 0 521 44503 5 hardback
ISBN 0 521 44952 9 paperback

**Transferred to
Digital Reprinting 1999**

**Printed in the
United States of America**

'Over himself, over his own body and mind, the individual is sovereign'.

John Stuart Mill

'No one outside of him can really touch him, can touch his soul, his immortality; he must live with himself forever. He has a depth within him unfathomable, an infinite abyss of existence'.

John Henry Newman

Contents

1
Introduction

Issues in health ethics or medical ethics or so-called bioethics are very often considered in abstraction from the social and political context in which they arise. But it is obvious that making decisions about those issues will differ quite radically in a liberal democratic society as compared with any kind of non-liberal society, whether it be theocratic or authoritarian (the term is used in a neutral sense) or paternalistic or 'traditional'. In a liberal society personal autonomy, the right to choose one's own way of life for oneself, is the supreme value. Certain consequences follow from the primacy given to personal autonomy in the liberal society. First, there is in such a society a sharp disjunction between the sphere of personal morality and the sphere of the law. The law is not concerned with matters of personal morality and the 'enforcement of morals'. Second, the liberal society is characterised by ethical pluralism, which allows a wide variety of ethical and religious (and non-religious) positions to be held by its members. Third, apart from the commitment to the primacy of personal autonomy, there is no determinate social consensus about a set of 'core values' or a 'public morality' which it is the law's business to safeguard and promote.

One might expect that in a liberal society the value of personal autonomy would be central in ethical discussions about new procreative technologies and modes of family formation; the limits of medical treatment and whether or not there is a 'right to die'; genetic intervention in human life; and so on. One might expect also that a clear distinction would be made between the morality of such issues and their legality: that is, whether or not the law should intervene to forbid them or control them. Again, one would think that ethical pluralism, particularly in the field of reproductive technology, would be not merely tolerated but positively welcomed and encouraged. However, what we find in fact is that many ethical positions proposed in this area are often in conflict with the values that are the heart of the liberal society.

Over many years I have served on a number of committees concerned with medical ethics and bioethical issues, and I have often been astonished by the way some committee members on occasion adopt quite authoritarian and paternalistic positions wholly at odds with the values of the liberal society of which they are a part. Under the guise of ensuring the 'common good' or defending 'public policy' or a set of 'core values' without which, it is claimed, civilised society will collapse, they are quite prepared, in the most authoritarian way, to tell people what is good for them and to lay down prohibitions about what they may and may not do with their lives. When one remonstrates with them that we are supposed to be living in a liberal society where individual autonomy and personal liberty are the central values, these people usually reply that liberty is one thing but licence is another and that 'libertarianism' should not be confused with true liberalism!

St Augustine remarks in his *Confessions* that in his unregenerate youth he prayed to God, 'Give me chastity, but not yet'. In much the same way many people in our society say in effect: 'Give me liberty, but not too much'. They acknowledge the values of the liberal society but they are unwilling to pursue them seriously and consistently, and to press them to their logical conclusions. As a nineteenth century thinker once said: such people think that moral principles can be summoned up and dismissed very much as we summon up and dismiss a hansom cab.

This is, alas, especially the case with some Christians who seem to think that they have a right to use the law to enforce Christian morality on divorce, abortion, contraception, assisted procreation, suicide and so on. I am myself a Christian and I have always thought that, while upholding their own moral values, Christians should also be especially concerned to uphold the value of personal autonomy. There has been a long tradition of Christian theological thought (more honoured, perhaps, in the breach than in the observance) which emphasises the primacy of the individual 'conscience'. St Thomas Aquinas says, for example, that it is a sin to go against the dictates of one's conscience. Again, it has always been a tenet of traditional Christianity that it is a sin to coerce non-Christians into the Christian Church, and one may legitimately infer that it is similarly against Christian faith to use the law to coerce non-believers in respect of moral matters.

The Catholic Church, of course, claims that its opposition to abortion, contraception, assisted procreation and the like is based not on specifically religious grounds but on the 'natural law' which is accessible to everyone regardless of his or her religion. But the natural law theory of ethics is one theory among a number of competing philosophical theories of ethics and it must take its chance, so to speak, among them. It represents one ethical position among the plurality of ethical positions that characterises the liberal society and it cannot claim any special or privileged place or status. In any case, there are widely differing interpretations, even among supporters of the theory, as to what the natural law recommends or forbids.

Whilst the view of the supremacy of conscience and personal liberty just mentioned has always been implicit in Christian moral theology, the tragedy has been that until very recently it has not been fully exploited by Christian thinkers. Nietzsche says somewhere that if Christians are redeemed they ought to look rather more as though they were redeemed! In much the same way, if, as Christians claim, the truth has really made them free, they ought to start behaving as though they were lovers of freedom.

Some think, mistakenly, that liberalism involves some kind of ethical relativism or scepticism, which would mean that no one ethical or moral position was better than any other. But liberalism is not based on ethical relativism or scepticism and it does not deny that people may espouse positions which are, objectively speaking, morally right. What is of the essence of liberalism is the moral conviction that, because they are autonomous moral agents or persons, people must as far as possible be free to choose for themselves, even if their choices are, objectively speaking, mistaken; and further that the state may not impose one moral or religious position on the whole community but, so long as they do not violate or harm the personal autonomy of others, must treat all such positions equally. As one of the contemporary champions of the liberal ideal, Ronald Dworkin, says: liberalism 'cannot be based on scepticism. Its constitutive morality provides that human beings must be treated as equals by their government, not because there is no right or wrong in political morality, but because that is what is right'.[1]

Christians then, or anyone else for that matter, may quite properly maintain and promote their own moral position on the issues to be discussed here, but if they are citizens of a liberal society they will not merely tolerate but respect the conscientious right of their fellow citizens to hold contrary moral positions, and they will not seek to have their own views imposed by the state. The same point has been nicely made by an eminent American moral theologian, Richard A. McCormick SJ. A Christian ethicist working in the area of public policy, he says, 'should bring his/her convictions to the public table — even those nourished by religious faith — but also his/her sense of realism. For me, that realism means that my moral convictions are inherently intelligible. But it also means the willingness to acknowledge at some point that others may not think so'.[2] The notion of the liberal society proposed in this book is, it goes without saying, controversial in that, first, there are different and competing versions of the liberal ideal and, second, there have been radical criticisms of it by some contemporary thinkers. However, while I cannot enter into a detailed defence of my version of the liberal ideal, I believe that a defence can be given.[3] My version is, as will be apparent, an 'ideal type' and I do not claim that any particular society actually exemplifies or embodies that ideal. At the same time I believe that my view of the liberal society represents the essential features of that new conception of society that began in the eighteenth century with Kant and others, was later developed by Mill and other nineteenth century thinkers, and was further elaborated by contemporary liberal thinkers such as John Rawls, Isaiah Berlin, Ronald Dworkin and Joseph Raz.

In parenthesis, I might mention that the idea of the liberal society put forward in this book is not necessarily linked with the idea of limited or minimal government intervention (a night-watchman state) nor with economic *laissez faire*. In my view the government in a liberal society has an obligation not merely to prevent, in a negative way, restrictions on the exercise of personal autonomy, but actively and positively to promote the socio-economic conditions within which personal freedom and autonomy can flourish. People cannot act in an authentically free and autonomous way if they live in dire poverty or in conditions of social anarchy, or if they do not have basic education and do not enjoy basic health. Equally, they cannot be autonomous agents if they do not have the opportunity to make real choices.

To forestall a possible objection: this does not mean that the state is involved in playing a moral role in the sense that it is promoting, and enforcing, one specific kind of morality. For the state to promote conditions of personal autonomy, so that people are able to choose freely their own styles of life, is not the same as coercing people to be moral in a specific way.

I am principally concerned here with the set of ethical issues that have come up in the sphere of health generally, medicine more specifically and biotechnology even more particularly, within a liberal democratic (and ethically pluralistic) society, and with the ways in which the community in such a society can face up to those issues. In order to keep the discussion within manageable bounds I have focussed on a relatively limited set of medical–ethical and bioethical issues. First, I discuss questions about the ending or termination of human life (usually placed under the misleading rubric of 'euthanasia'). Second, I consider the issues concerned with the new and alternative ways of assisted reproduction and family formation, and finally with the complex set of ethical questions involved in the distribution of health-care resources. Each of those areas involves a number of other subsidiary issues, from the meaning of 'the quality of human life' to the right of women to control their reproductive capacities, to the adequacy of utilitarian approaches in health-care resource allocation.

The idea of personal autonomy, with all its connotations, plays a central part in the analysis of those issues and I hope to show how important and how powerful that concept is in bioethical discussion. No doubt a complete ethics cannot be generated from the idea of autonomy: nonetheless a great deal of ethical capital can be extracted from it. In recent US medical ethics the concept of autonomy has, to some extent, fallen out of favour and been subjected to sharp criticism because it has been linked with an excessively individualistic and self-regarding position. However, I argue that an emphasis on personal autonomy can go together with an altruistic concern for others and with a recognition of community values. A person may very well make a conscientious and autonomous moral decision about her or his responsibilities and obligations towards others. Of course, the concept of autonomy may be used by some people in the service of an ideology of atomistic individualism, but there is no necessary connection between the two.

A further point: although Mill and some other supporters of the liberal ideal purport to justify it in utilitarian terms — the principle of individual liberty leads to the most beneficial social consequences — there is no essential link between the liberal ideal and the theory of utilitarianism. In fact, personal autonomy is an 'absolute' value or intrinsic good regardless of any consequences it may have, and it is for that reason that a utilitarian justification is inadequate.

After an introductory chapter, in chapter 2 the ethical values presupposed by a liberal society are discussed. The primacy of personal autonomy is analysed, as are its consequences — antipaternalism, the distinction between the sphere of law and the sphere of personal morality, ethical pluralism and what a moral 'consensus' means in a society of autonomous agents. Recent criticisms of the liberal ideal are considered and a reply in defence of liberal values is given. Finally, the relevance of those values for contemporary bioethical issues is discussed.

In chapter 3 the following questions are posed. Can we choose, in the name of autonomy, to die when we judge that our continued survival is humanly pointless or that the quality of our future life is likely to be zero? Can we refuse medical treatment to, or withdraw treatment from, patients when their future quality of life is likely to be minimal? This involves a discussion of whether we can impute 'consent' to incompetent patients (disabled newborn children, the comatose, those in persistent vegetative states and so on) who are incapable of giving consent to withdrawal of treatment. Again, the notion of quality of life is an ambiguous one. Some speak as though a person's quality of life can be measured objectively and even quantified. As against this I argue that quality of life can be defined only by reference to the notion of personal autonomy. The question we have to ask is: will the person in question be able to exercise some minimal degree of autonomous control over his or her life if treatment is successful?

In the following chapter the different modes of birth and family formation made possible by new reproductive technologies are considered, as is the 'right to procreative liberty'. By way of example, an extensive analysis and discussion of surrogacy arrangements is provided. Once again, if the principle of autonomy is to be employed consistently, women should be allowed, in certain circumstances, to be surrogate mothers if they freely choose to do so. The various criticisms of these technologies are discussed and particular attention is given to certain feminist thinkers (for example Corea and Rowland) who claim that the new forms of assisted procreation do not enhance women's autonomy but lead to their oppression. I argue that the feminist principle that women have the right to control their own bodies (a form of the principle of autonomy) applies here in the same way that it applies with regard to abortifacient and contraceptive technologies. One cannot logically use the principle with regard to the latter technologies and then reject it with regard to reproductive technologies.

In chapter 5 I discuss the ethical dimensions of the present debate over the distribution of scarce health-care resources. The debate has been dominated by utilitarian approaches and I attempt to show how inadequate they are with respect to the justice or fairness of health-care resource allocation. Again, utilitarian, economic rationalist and cost–benefit oriented models tend to be *dirigiste* and paternalistic, and neglect both patient autonomy and the professional autonomy of physicians and health-care workers. So called 'community consultation' (as in the Oregon scheme described in chapter 5) is limited to establishing and ranking health-care priorities on a cost–benefit basis. Patient choices are not enhanced or enlarged but are in fact severely restricted in the name of cost–benefit efficiency. I argue that in a liberal society the enhancement of patient choice and control of medical resources, and of professional autonomy, should be major goals of any allocation or distribution scheme. This approach sets severe limits to 'rational' planning in this area and indicates the need for a 'piecemeal social engineering' strategy which will respect the values associated with autonomy.

In a final chapter I consider the liberal ideal as against the realities of current medical–ethical and bioethical discussion and practice, and also whether any kind of consensus about bioethical and medical–ethical questions is possible in a liberal, ethically pluralistic, multicultural society of autonomous individuals.

NOTES

1. Ronald Dworkin, *Law's Empire*, Cambridge, Mass., Harvard University Press, 1986, p.441.
2. Richard A. McCormick, *The Critical Calling: Reflections on Moral Dilemmas since Vatican II*, Washington, Georgetown University Press, 1989.
3. See, for example, Joseph Raz, *The Morality of Freedom*, Oxford, Clarendon Press, 1980.

2
Autonomy and the Liberal Ideal

The idea of autonomy

The idea of autonomy is a blindingly obvious one. It simply means that if I am to act in an ethical or moral way I must choose for myself what I am going to do. I may of course take advice from others and I may be subject to persuasion and pressure from external sources, but when the chips are down I must decide and choose for myself. Only then is what I have done imputable to me so that it is *my* act, and only then am I responsible for it and praiseworthy or blameworthy for it.[1] As a contemporary thinker has put it:

> While we may be mistaken in our beliefs about value, it doesn't follow that someone else, who has reason to believe a mistake has been made, can come along and improve my life by leading it for me, in accordance with the correct account of value. On the contrary, no life goes better by being led from the outside according to values the person doesn't endorse. My life only goes better if I'm leading it from the inside, according to my beliefs about value. Praying to God may be a valuable activity, but you have to believe that it's a worthwhile thing to do — that it has some worthwhile point and purpose. You can coerce someone into going to church and making the right physical movements, but you won't make someone's life better that way. It won't work, even if the coerced

person is mistaken in her belief that praying to God is a waste of time. It won't work because a valuable life has to be a life led from the inside.[2]

The idea of moral autonomy has had a long history in Western thought. The germs of the idea are present in Aristotle's discussion of 'voluntary action' in the *Nicomachean Ethics*: a moral act is one that is deliberated upon and freely chosen by the agent.[3] It received further elaboration in a discussion of 'conscience' by medieval philosophers from Peter Lombard through Philip the Chancellor and St Bonaventure to St Thomas Aquinas.[4] For these philosophers the central question was whether a judgment of conscience could be binding or obligatory on a person. Aquinas, drawing on this tradition of thought, gave the surprising answer that if one sincerely believed and decided, after serious reflection, that a given line of action was objectively right, even though in fact it was objectively wrong, then one was bound to follow that decision.[5] Aquinas qualified this position by saying that there are some matters which everyone is presumed, even bound, to know to be wrong, so that if one believed them not to be wrong one would be culpably ignorant 'since the error arises from ignorance of the Divine Law which he is bound to know'. But on other matters my conscience binds or obliges me.[6] As one commentator has explained Aquinas' position:

> The ruling principle is clear; a man who acts against his conscience is always in the wrong, even if his conscience is mistaken. If he acts according to his conscience and his conscience is right, well and good; if his conscience is mistaken but through no fault of his own, then his action is not morally bad.[7]

In the nineteenth century, Cardinal Newman also drew upon this tradition of thought. In the English controversy over whether Catholics' allegiance to the Pope conflicted with their allegiance to the Queen, Newman affirms the right of personal conscience. Thus in the *Letter to the Duke of Norfolk* Newman says that as a Catholic and an Englishman he owes allegiance both to the Queen and the Pope and it may happen, though it will be a rare occurrence, that the two allegiances conflict with each other. In such an event, Newman says, 'I should decide according to the particular case which is beyond all rules, and must be decided on its merits'. I may get advice from others, but 'if, after all, I could not take their view of the matter, then I must rule myself by my own judgment and my conscience'. Newman concludes with the flamboyant statement: 'Certainly, if I am obliged to bring religion into after-dinner toasts (which indeed does not seem quite the thing) I shall drink — to the Pope, if you please — still to Conscience first and the Pope afterwards'.[8] Behind this view of conscience lies a philosophical view of the human person which Newman expresses in a magnificent passage in *Parochial and Plain Sermons*. 'No one', he says, 'outside of him can really touch him, can touch his soul, his immortality; he must live with himself forever. He has a depth within him unfathomable, an infinite abyss of existence'.[9]

The idea of personal autonomy is, perhaps, most famously linked with the name of Immanuel Kant. In a sense the whole of Kant's moral philosophy revolves around the idea that the moral agent is her or his own law-giver. By my reason I discern the 'categorical imperatives' or absolute obligations or duties of the moral law and I impose them on myself. If I act because of any non-rational motive — my feelings or inclinations or the coercive force of others — then I am no longer acting ethically or morally. For Kant, the autonomous moral agent is not just the source of moral value but is intrinsically valuable in herself and must be respected as such by others. She is an end-in-itself and can never be used solely as an instrumental means for achieving the ends or purposes of another. To treat another person as a means to one's own ends is in effect to treat her as a thing. With Kant we witness a development of the idea of autonomy from being a fundamental condition of ethical action to being an ethical value in its own right and as such deserving of moral respect.[10]

It has been argued that the idea of personal autonomy is distinct from Kant's idea that we are both the authors and the subjects of self-enacted moral principles. For Kant, this critic says, the moral subject's 'authorship [of his life] reduced itself to a vanishing point as it allowed only one set of principles which people can rationally legislate, and they are the same for all'.[11] But Kant also defines the moral subject/agent or person as an 'end in itself' that can never be treated merely as a means to some further end. There is, no doubt, an unresolved tension in Kant's thought between the idea that there is a set of 'categorical imperatives' (absolute and universal moral principles) imposed on me by my reason (where the authorship of my life is indeed reduced to vanishing point), and his idea that I am, as a moral agent, an autonomous 'end in itself' who alone has the responsibility of determining the direction and shape of my moral life (where the authorship of my moral life is given full recognition). As we shall see later, this tension is particularly evident in Kant's discussion of suicide.

Of course, the freedom to choose, which is of the essence of personal autonomy, is freedom to choose some concrete line of action which we believe to be morally good. Autonomy does not mean choosing simply for choosing's sake. But that does not imply, as some have argued, that freedom to choose has no ethical value in itself but only becomes valuable in the light of the concrete actions chosen: in other words, it is because *those actions* are good, or believed to be good, that freedom to choose and autonomy are good. However, autonomy, the capacity for self-determination, is also valuable in itself in the sense that, even though *what* I choose (the content of my act) is objectively bad, my choosing it is still good in that it is a free and autonomous act as opposed to one that is coerced. If we contrast two acts: (a) one that is freely chosen but objectively wrong, and (b) one that is coerced and not freely chosen, but which is also objectively good, the liberal will say that the first act is more morally valuable than the second.

One might also mention that freedom of expression or 'free

speech' is based upon the recognition that members of a liberal society have a right to be treated as autonomous moral agents who must be allowed to decide for themselves the worth of views expressed to them. There are of course cases (defamatory statements, racial vilification and the like) where the expression of certain views may cause direct injury or harm to other people and violate their personal autonomy. In such cases the state may intervene. But if a government intervenes to curb free speech on the grounds that people may be morally depraved or corrupted by the views that are expressed, or led into politically questionable behaviour, or persuaded to believe false (religious or other) ideas, it is in effect treating its citizens as children lacking full autonomy who are not capable of considering those views for themselves and making their own judgments on them.

No doubt, as Mill was to argue, freedom of expression may also be justified on the ground that it leads to beneficial consequences overall. Thus we are more likely to discover the truth, whether in religion, politics or any other sphere, through free and untrammelled debate where a variety of views are able to be expressed. But this consequentialist justification is much weaker than that which sees freedom of expression as a corollary of the recognition of the value of personal autonomy. The best that the consequentialist justification of free speech can allow is that in most circumstances it is likely to be the case that free speech will bring about more good social effects than bad. It is incapable of according an absolute value to freedom of expression.

Much later on, philosophers such as Jean-Paul Sartre attempted to construct a whole ethical theory around the idea of autonomy. Thus for Sartre the conscious subject has no predetermined 'essence' or make-up or 'nature' but is wholly self-determining. I make myself through my choices and I am totally responsible for myself. The realisation of this is the basis of the first Sartrean ethical commandment: always act as one who is self-determining and responsible for what one does. This is what Sartre calls the attitude of 'authenticity'. The negative corollary of this is that I must not try to evade my freedom of self-determination, and my responsibility for making myself through my acts, by practising 'self deception' or 'bad faith' (*mauvaise foi*). The attempt to escape the 'burden' of freedom and self-determination or autonomy is paradoxical, since any attempt to abdicate from having to choose freely and responsibly for myself presupposes that I am free. I am in effect saying: 'I freely choose no longer to freely choose what I am going to do', cr 'As a conscious self-determining subject I choose to be a predetermined thing'. Just as for Descartes I cannot doubt that I am a conscious being since I have to presuppose that I am conscious in order to doubt, so also for Sartre the attempt to abandon one's moral autonomy presupposes that I am free, self-determining and autonomous. Nevertheless, as Sartre shows in his brilliant delineations of the pathological strategies of 'bad faith' and 'self-deception' in all areas of human life, we can certainly succeed in deceiving ourselves and in forsaking our autonomy and evading responsibility for ourselves. In fact, for Sartre the life of 'authenticity' based upon autonomy is arduous and only rarely successful. In a sense Sartre deromanticises the idea of autonomy in that, while emphasising that it is the central good, he also emphasises that it is a burden which most people would prefer to avoid and that it is very difficult to escape from the lures of 'bad faith' and to achieve authenticity. We all say that we want to be free and autonomous ('Give me liberty or death'!) but in fact we spend most of our time trying to escape from freedom and autonomy.[12]

The liberal society

The relevance of the idea of autonomy for liberal democracy is obvious. The idea is of course at the basis of the ideas of political 'liberty' and 'the rights of man' in eighteenth century political thought. However, it was not until nineteenth century thinkers such as John Stuart Mill that a political theory based on moral autonomy was formally developed. Put briefly, the ideal of a liberal society is based upon the principle of personal liberty, namely that, to the greatest degree possible, people should be free to make their own life-choices and decisions for themselves and that, as a corollary, the state, acting through the law, should as far as possible opt out of the province of personal morality. In other words, it is not the business of the state, or the law, to make us virtuous, or to enforce personal morality, or to establish a common morality. The liberal society is one in which to the maximum degree people are at liberty to exercise their personal autonomy. By way of contrast, in quasi-authoritarian or theo-cratic or traditional societies personal autonomy is subordinated to 'objective' moral values as declared by 'the authorities'. In this view, the important thing is to do what is objectively good, not to choose for oneself, and the emphasis is on one's duties or obli-gations and not on one's rights which are deemed to be 'indi-vidualistic' and potentially anti-social. If one autonomously chooses to do what one ought to do, that is a bonus. Most people do not know what is good for them and they must be told, and led, to do what is good. Paternalism is therefore an inescapable and necessary feature of the social and political process.

The ideal of the liberal society was given its classic formula-tion in John Stuart Mill's essay *On Liberty*. The principle which enables us to demarcate the sphere of individual liberty from that of the state and the law, and to set limits to the latter is this:

> The only purpose for which power can be rightfully exercised over any member of a civilised community, against his will, is to prevent harm to others. His own good, either physical or moral, is not a sufficient warrant. He cannot rightfully be compelled to do or for-bear because it will be better for him to do so, because it will make him happier, because, in the opinions of others to do so would be wise, or even right. These are good reasons for remonstrating with him, or reasoning with him, or persuading him, or entreating him, but not for compelling him, or visiting him with any evil in case he do otherwise. . . . The only part of the conduct of any one, for which he is amenable to society, is that which concerns others. In the part which merely concerns himself, his independence is, of right,

16

absolute. Over himself, over his own body and mind, the individual is sovereign.[13]

Only if a person's acts directly harm other people and prevent or inhibit the exercise of their personal liberty may the state, through the law, intervene.

Mill admits, of course, that there may be occasions when the state, through the law, might legitimately override the autonomy of individuals for their own good. However, in a liberal democratic society that kind of paternalism should be limited to situations where it is clearly justified, and the onus is always on the state to show that it is in the long-term interests of those whose autonomy is being overridden in the short term. Put in another way, the sphere of personal liberty should be maximised and the sphere of paternalistic action by the state should be progressively minimised. (As we saw before, that maximisation of personal liberty and autonomy may very well involve intervention by the state to promote socio-economic conditions within which personal autonomy can flourish.)

A consequence of this is that there is a strict disjunction between the two spheres of personal morality and state intervention. Certain kinds of behaviour may be immoral, sinful or ethically undesirable, but the state should prohibit them only if they involve harm being done to others. Prostitution, for example, would generally be thought to be morally undesirable but that by itself is no reason for legally prohibiting it. As the UK Wolfenden Committee (full of Millian milk) put it in 1957, apropos of the decriminalisation of prostitution and homosexual acts between consenting adults, it is not 'the function of the law to intervene in the private lives of citizens, or to seek to enforce any particular pattern of behaviour'. And again, 'unless a deliberate attempt be made by society, acting through the agency of the law, to equate the sphere of crime with that of sin, there must remain a realm of private morality and immorality which is, in brief and crude terms, not the law's business'. By decriminalising certain acts such as prostitution or abortion the state is not thereby approving them: it is simply declaring that these acts fall within the area of private morality and that this is out of bounds for state intervention and the criminal law.[14]

A further consequence of the Millian view of the liberal society is that it is possible to have a society without any substantive agreement or consensus on basic moral and religious values. Traditional or religiously based societies have usually exacted agreement on a set of 'core values' — belonging to a particular religion, adhering to certain sexual taboos, accepting a certain form of marital and family life and so on — to which all the members of these societies are supposed to give assent and allegiance. However the liberal society claims that, at least ideally, members of society are required only to agree that personal liberty or autonomy is the supreme value. In a sense this is an agreement to disagree, in other words for each to tolerate the personal worldview and value system of the other so long as they do not infringe upon one's own or others' freedom to follow out their own way of life. In such a society, social diversity and cultural pluralism are not seen as threats to the ethical 'consensus' that is supposed to underlie the social fabric; rather they are positively welcomed and encouraged, and seen as an index of social vitality. On the other hand, religiously based and traditional societies are, ideally at least, monocultural, and so-called multiculturalism is seen a a threat to social unity. Indeed, it is argued that a multicultural society is a contradiction in terms.

It was noted before that liberalism does not involve any kind of ethical relativism or scepticism, as though there were no objective values and it was in some way improper for members of a liberal society to espouse and propagate their own ethical or moral positions. In *On Liberty* Mill expressly rejects any kind of scepticism about ethical values and contemporary defenders of the liberal ideal do the same.[15] Liberalism in fact depends upon a recognition of the unequivocally objective value of personal autonomy and the other values — equality, justice and so on —

associated with it. Again, it recognises the right of individuals to maintain and actively propagate their own ethical positions. In fact, the freedom to choose can be seen as a necessary condition for overcoming subjectivism and attaining 'objectivity' in moral decision-making, in that it provides the opportunity for gathering relevant information and for the critical assessment of alternatives. Far from being motivated by a view that ethical decisions are subjective or arbitrary, it is motivated by the desire to overcome subjectivism and arbitrariness in the making of ethical decisions.[16]

At the same time, as we have seen, the liberal society, by virtue of its commitment to the value of autonomy, draws a sharp distinction between the sphere of personal moral views and the sphere of state intervention and the law. And that means that no members of a liberal society may invoke the law to impose their particular moral views on others.

In *On Liberty* John Stuart Mill talks a good deal about what he calls 'individuality'. In one sense this is identical with the idea of autonomy, the capacity of each person to pursue her or his life in an original and spontaneous way as an independent and self-determining moral agent. Defined in this way, individuality is something intrinsically good and society is best where this is promoted to the highest degree: that is, where the maximum number of people make their own free and responsible decisions. What does it profit a society in which everyone is coerced to do what is objectively right, if they do not choose to do it for themselves? Although, as we said before, some degree of paternalism may be justified in a society (for example, ensuring that children receive basic education whatever their wishes or choices) the ideal state of affairs would be one in which people freely choose to do what they ought to do. From this point of view, the state should always view its interventions in matters of personal morality as a necessary evil and something to be progressively diminished. In Mill's society the function of the law, one might say, is to create the conditions which will lead to its becoming less and less concerned with the enforcement of personal morality and so allow more and more scope to 'individuality'. As a contemporary Millian has said: 'The government has an obligation to create an environment providing individuals with an adequate range of options and the opportunities to choose them'.[17]

The liberty to decide and choose for oneself is, however, only part of what Mill means by 'individuality'. He also means the right to be different. Though this might be superficially interpreted as a plea for bohemianism or mere eccentricity, Mill is getting at something important here, namely that each person has his or her own moral style of life or 'vocation'. Morality is not just a matter of conforming to universal rules or following a maxim which, as Kant puts it, can apply to everyone alike. There is a saying that the saints are admirable but not imitable. But in a certain sense this is true of every moral agent. Each person has an inimitable moral style and vocation, and all his or her acts bear a distinctive personal impress.

As was said before, with Kant autonomy is no longer just a condition of moral action, as it was with Aristotle and medieval thinkers such as Aquinas, but becomes a value in itself. The same is true of Mill; for him individuality is an intrinsic good that should be respected and pursued for its own sake. Speaking of the recognition of individuality as a genuine development in moral consciousness, Isaiah Berlin has said:

> It may be that the ideal of freedom to live as one wishes — and the pluralism of values connected with it — is only the late fruit of our declining capitalist civilisation: an ideal which remote ages and primitive societies have not known, and which posterity will regard with curiosity, even sympathy, but little comprehension. This may be so, but no sceptical conclusion seems to me to follow. Principles are no less sacred because their duration cannot be guaranteed.[18]

Critics of the liberal ideal

This vision of a society of autonomous moral agents choosing freely for themselves, and willingly tolerating a situation of

moral or ethical pluralism on the basis of their commitment to
the value of liberty or moral autonomy, has been subjected, over
the last thirty years, to a sustained critique from various quar-
ters. There have been, first, attacks on the notion of autonomy
itself: for example that it grossly overestimates the capacity of
people to make decisions for themselves and neglects the degree
to which every human decision is influenced by both external
and internal (psychological) factors. Thus it has been said that
we are inescapably part of a particular community and that
communal values and practices largely set our ethical goals for
us. We discover them and do not deliberately choose them. This
is especially the case in so-called 'traditional' societies where the
whole idea of autonomous individuals choosing their life pro-
jects and engaging in what Mill calls their own 'experiments in
living' is, so it is claimed, absurd.[19] In this view autonomy is a
philosopher's myth with no meaning in practical life. Further,
Mill's emphasis on autonomy is said to be individualistic and
a-social in that it abstracts the individual from the social and
cultural context which gives human actions meaning and significance. Once again, this kind of atomistic individualism is said
to be a philosopher's fiction. No one lives like that. There is no
pre-social or a-social self because the self is always 'situated'
within a concrete set of social and cultural circumstances within
which in turn it has certain roles (I am a female or a male, a
father or a mother, a parent or a child, a worker or a professional, a Christian or a Muslim) and in terms of which it is
'defined'. In this sense the self is always a 'social construction'.
Allied with this objection, there is the charge that emphasis on
autonomy leads to a self-regarding ethical approach where the
rights of the individual against the state and other individuals
become central and the other-regarding responsibilities and
obligations of the individual are no longer important.

These criticisms are, however, misconceived. All that they
show is that the concept of autonomy, like all concepts, has a
'grey area' of application in practice. We know that on occasion
people, whatever their cultural situation and whatever external

forces influence them, are able to make considered and conscientious decisions for themselves and we can point to paradigm cases of such decisions. We can also point to paradigm cases of decisions that were so determined by external (social and cultural) and internal (psychological) factors that they were not decisions for which the agent could be held responsible or praised or blamed. In between there are the cases where it may not be completely clear whether or not an autonomous decision was made and whether or not responsibility for the decision should be imputed to the person involved. But the existence of such cases in the grey area does not mean that the concept of autonomy is vacuous. As Dr Johnson once remarked: just because there is a zone of twilight it does not follow that we cannot distinguish between day and night. Unless one is prepared to argue, on some kind of socio-cultural deterministic grounds, that it is impossible in traditional societies for people to make moral or ethical decisions for which they are responsible and thus deserving of praise or blame, it must be possible to make autonomous decisions.

While it is true that the self is always 'situated' it does not follow that it is wholly *determined* by its situation or roles: it is what I *do* with my given situation and roles and what I *make* of them by my choices that make me into a self. As a self-determining agent I may freely choose to stay with and live out the roles and the situation in which I find myself, or I may freely choose to break with and change that situation, and take on radically new roles. In traditional societies, the opportunity or space for such alternative self-determining choices and 'conversions' is severely limited. The liberal society, however, is one which promotes and provides space for these self-determining choices to the greatest possible degree.

As for the criticism that the notion of autonomy is linked to an individualistic and a-social stance, there is absolutely no reason why an autonomous act must necessarily be self-regarding in intent and cannot be other-regarding. People may very well make conscientious and autonomous moral decisions about

22

their responsibilities and obligations towards others and acknowledge their dependency on others. A society of autonomous agents is not necessarily a collection of individualistic, self-contained and self-regarding atoms or 'islands of self-conviction and self-direction'.[20]

Other objections have been made about what is claimed to be the paradoxical character of the very idea of the liberal society, namely that it is possible to have a society without any kind of social consensus or, put in another way, that the 'common good' of the liberal society is that it has no common good.[21] But in fact there is no paradox. It is true that in a liberal society there is no common good of a substantive kind; but there is a common good centred on the values of liberty, autonomy and moral diversity. It is worthwhile citing here the words of an American legal scholar, Judith Shklar, apropos of Lord Justice Devlin's famous criticism in 1965 of the Wolfenden Committee report on homosexuality and prostitution.[22] Devlin had argued that the law *is* in practice inescapably concerned with matters of private morality and that it *ought* to be so concerned since agreement on certain basic and substantive moral values is necessary for there to be a society at all. By definition a society is a group of people who are agreed upon a set of fundamental moral values. To the question 'how do we know what these values are?', Devlin had replied that they are known by the average member of the community, that is, as the English legal fiction put it, by 'the man on the Clapham omnibus'. Referring to Devlin's 'contention that society will fall apart unless an accepted morality is enforced by the public authorities', Shklar comments ironically:

The tricky question of who really knows what is moral is answered by referring the doubter to 'the man on the Clapham bus' whose moral attitudes can be taken as representative of all England, or at least of all of England that matters. Here one is in the presence of the mythical 'average man' whose uses have at last been discovered by conservatives. The unquestioning mind is taken as the best index of public opinion, morality is then identified with this opinion, and the survival of society is made to depend upon its being the sole guide

23

for public policy ... That tolerance and freedom might also be values, that the moral successes of public enforcement remain dubious, are matters which do not even seem to occur to this type of mentality.

Shklar concludes by saying:

Freedom and diversity are values too, and individualism and impersonal justice are types of morality as well. To defend them is not to deny the obvious — that, whatever 'society' does, it promotes some set of values. However, the defenders of 'the man on the Clapham bus' not only are urging upon us a very specific and narrow set of norms; they are doing it in order to bring conformity into a pluralistic society, and under the false pretence of defending moral values against the amoral.[23]

The same reply might also be made to the criticism that the state and the law cannot be neutral with respect to moral values. Thus a recent critic of the 'liberal political-philosophical project' argues that there is no neutral vantage point from which legislators, judges and the like can stand and rationally arbitrate the conflicts between those with different moral stances. 'One can', he says, 'participate in politics and law ... only as a partisan of particular moral/religious convictions about the human'.[24] In one sense that is true, but it neglects the fact that a commitment to moral autonomy, and to the ethical pluralism that goes with it, is not at all like a commitment to a particular and 'partisan' moral stance. An agreement on the supreme value of autonomy is precisely an agreement to disagree about substantive and partisan moral positions. In that sense it is a meta-partisan stance.

Difficulties arise of course when a liberal society contains minority groups which reject the very notion of autonomy and all that it involves. In effect they bite the hand that tolerates them by rejecting the basis of the liberty that is extended to them and that enables them to exist. What we have here is a situation where two competing and incompatible views of

24

society are in conflict and there is no way, *in principle*, to resolve that conflict. (A liberal society does not have to be absolutely neutral with regard to values and absolutely permissive of any and every group. As we have seen, the liberal society makes a commitment to the value of autonomy and it does not have to tolerate groups that contradict that value and all that flows from it.) Nevertheless, in practice it is often possible to negotiate with such groups and to secure acceptance of the values of the liberal society — autonomy, ethical and religious pluralism, the distinction between the law and personal morality — on pragmatic grounds.

Finally, the critics of the liberal society object that there is no place in it for genuinely communitarian values. Once again this relies upon the assumption that such a society is a collection of atomic self-regarding individuals. But we do not have to choose between, on the one hand, an acceptance of communitarian consensus and, on the other hand, rampant individualism where everyone does her or his own thing and where there is no place at all for community values. In effect the liberal society provides a space for a multiplicity of forms of community life: in fact, it encourages cultural diversity and sees it as an index of social vitality. What it denies is that community values can be legislated for and sanctioned by the state, and that there should be one monolithic set of such values which excludes or marginalises any kind of genuine diversity or pluralism. As Mill nicely puts it:

It would be a great misunderstanding of this doctrine (of the autonomy of the individual) to suppose that it is one of selfish indifference, which pretends that human beings have no business with each other's conduct in life, and that they should not concern themselves about the well-doing or well-being of one another, unless their own interest is involved. Instead of any diminution, there is need of a great increase of disinterested exertion to promote the good of others. But disinterested benevolence can find other instruments to persuade people to their good than whips and scourges, either of the literal or metaphorical sort . . . Human beings owe each other help

25

to distinguish the better from the worse, and encouragement to choose the former and avoid the latter. They should be ever stimulating each other to increased exercise of their higher faculties, and increased direction of their feelings and aims towards wise instead of foolish, elevating instead of degrading, objects and contemplations. But neither one person, nor any number of persons, is warranted in saying to another human creature of ripe years, that he shall not do with his life for his own benefit what he chooses to do with it.[25]

What is true in some of these criticisms of the liberal society is that it, like every social structure, has its own peculiar costs and benefits. In other words, the liberal society's emphasis on the value of personal autonomy and liberty, with all its consequences, is bought at a certain price. The sense of communal solidarity, so strong in traditional societies, is for example weakened (though not wholly abolished) in the liberal society, and the individual bears the full 'burden', as Sartre calls it, of ethical responsibility for his or her actions. The autonomous agents of the liberal society cannot seek the communal warmth and comfort of traditional societies and are bereft of the paternalistic guidance available in religiously based and authoritarian societies. (Though, of course, the advantages of such societies are bought at a considerable human cost: the lack of space for the exercise of personal liberty and the promotion of what Mill calls 'individuality', and the inhibition of intellectual, moral and political diversity and variety. This is something that latter-day 'traditionalists' prefer to forget.)

The liberal ideal, with its focus on individual liberty, social diversity and cultural pluralism, is difficult to maintain because it goes against the grain of our human tendency to escape the burdens of autonomous behaviour and to seek conformity and refuge in 'the crowd'. Thus we tend to invoke nostalgically the idea of a moral consensus on a set of core values that are supposed to be at the basis of our society and that are implicitly known and safeguarded by 'the community'. Of course, it can be interesting and valuable to know, if we can discover it, what members of the community think about policies at any one time. But in a liberal society, where a pluralism of values is not only tolerated but actively encouraged, there is no such thing as 'the community' view which has some kind of special normative status and which provides a basis for a public morality or for that nebulous entity which judges are fond of calling 'public policy'.

This then is the general context within which public ethical discussion, including medical ethics and bioethics, ought to be carried on in our society. Unfortunately, a good deal of this discussion takes place without any reference to this context and as a result there is constant confusion of the spheres of morality and the law; misunderstandings about the legitimacy of ethical pluralism; illusions about a 'public morality', so-called 'public policy' and the will of 'the community'; gross inconsistencies about people's rights; and so on. As I have already remarked, some of the stances adopted, especially in the fields of the ethics of assisted procreation and reproductive technology, the ethics of death and dying, and the ethics of health resource allocation are so authoritarian and paternalistic that one wonders if their supporters realise that they are supposed to be living in a liberal democratic society. It is the contention of this book that those engaged in bioethical discussion must become aware of the fact that they are living in a liberal society and take account of its basic values.

NOTES

1. On the concept of autonomy see Joseph Raz, *The Morality of Freedom*, Oxford, Clarendon Press, 1986, especially ch. 14, 'Autonomy and Pluralism' and ch.15, 'Freedom and Autonomy'; Robert Young, *Personal Autonomy; Beyond Negative and Positive Liberty*, The Hague, Croom Helm, 1986; G. Dworkin, *The Theory and Practice of Autonomy*, Cambridge, Cambridge University Press, 1988; J. Christman (ed.) *The Inner Citadel: Essays on Individual Autonomy*, New York, Oxford University Press, 1989.

2. Will Kymlicka, 'Liberalism and communitarianism', *Canadian Journal of Philosophy*, 18, 1988, p.183.
3. *Nicomachean Ethics*, Book III, ch.1.
4. See Timothy Potts, *Conscience in Medieval Philosophy*, Cambridge, Cambridge University Press, 1980, and Eric D'Arcy, *Conscience and Its Right to Freedom*, London, Sheed and Ward, 1961.
5. *Summa Theologiae*, 1a 2ae, q.19, art. 6.
6. ibid. art. 7
7. Thomas Gilby, *Summa Theologiae*, 1a 2ae, q.19, arts. 18–21, vol. 18, London, Blackfriars/Eyre and Spottiswoode, Appendix 15, p.182.
8. See Max Charlesworth, 'Newman on church, state and conscience', in *Church, State and Conscience*, St Lucia, Queensland University Press, 1973, p.3.
9. J.H. Newman, *Parochial and Plain Sermons*, vol. 4, Sermon VI, 'The Individuality of the Soul', London, Rivingtons, 1863, pp.82–3.
10. Immanuel Kant, *Foundation of the Metaphysics of Morals*, 1785, trans. Carl J. Friedrich, in *The Philosophy of Kant*, New York, Modern Library, 1949.
11. Joseph Raz, *The Morality of Freedom*, op. cit. p.370.
12. See Jean-Paul Sartre, *Existentialism and Humanism*, trans. P. Mairet, Brooklyn, Haskell House, 1977; and the section 'Patterns of bad faith' in *Being and Nothingness*, trans. Hazel Barnes, London, Methuen, 1969.
13. John Stuart Mill, *On Liberty*, R.B. McCallum (ed.), Oxford, Blackwell, 1946, pp.8–9.
14. *Report of the Committee on Homosexual Offences and Prostitution* (the Wolfenden Committee), London, HM Stationery Office 1957.
15. Mill, *On Liberty*, op. cit., pp.67–8. See also Ronald Dworkin, *Law's Empire*, Cambridge, Mass., Harvard University Press, 1986.
16. See Will Kymlicka, 'Liberalism and communitarianism', op. cit. p.185.
17. Joseph Raz, *The Morality of Freedom*, op. cit. pp.417–18.
18. I. Berlin, *Two Concepts of Liberty*, Oxford, Clarendon Press, 1958, p.57.
19. See Alasdair MacIntyre, *After Virtue: A Study in Moral Theory*, 2nd edn, London, Duckworth, 1986; Michael Sandel, *Liberalism and the Limits of Justice*, Cambridge, Cambridge University Press, 1982; Charles Taylor, *Hegel and Modern Society*, Cambridge, Cambridge University Press, 1979; Michael Walzer, *Spheres of Justice*, Oxford, Blackwell, 1985. For an excellent counter-critique see Will Kymlicka, 'Liberalism and communitarianism', op. cit. See also C. Kukathas and P. Pettit, *Rawls: A Theory of Justice and Its Critics*,

Cambridge, Polity Press, 1990, ch.6, 'The Communitarian Critique'.

20. Richard A. McCormick, *The Critical Calling: Reflections on Moral Dilemmas since Vatican II*, Washington, Georgetown University Press, 1989, p.220.

21. For a recent survey of these criticisms see Stephen Macedo, *Liberal Values: Citizenship, Virtue and Community in Liberal Constitutionalism*, Oxford, Clarendon Press, 1990.

22. Patrick Devlin, *The Enforcement of Morals*, Oxford, Oxford University Press, 1965.

23. Judith Shklar, *Legalism*, Cambridge, Mass., Harvard University Press, 1964, pp.90-1.

24. Michael J. Perry, *Morality, Politics and the Law*, New York, Oxford University Press, 1988, p.183.

25. Mill, *On Liberty*, pp.67-8.

3
Ending Life

The ethics of suicide

In the *Foundation of the Metaphysics of Morals* Kant asks himself whether a person may, in certain circumstances, take his life when he judges that his continued existence is humanly pointless. Surprisingly, the great apostle of personal autonomy holds that such a person would be acting immorally. Kant argues that one contemplating suicide is caught in a 'contradiction' in that he is, on the one hand, concerned to promote his self-interest by seeking to escape further suffering or dying in a situation where he has lost control over himself and become a 'vegetable'; but on the other hand he wishes, by taking his life, to abolish his 'self' and all possibility of securing his future self-interest. Since what is contradictory is irrational, suicide is irrational. Kant also develops another argument to the effect that a person deciding to commit suicide sees the taking of his life as a means to an end (the cessation of suffering, the avoidance of an 'undignified' death). He no longer sees himself as an autonomous moral agent (or person) deserving of absolute moral respect, or as an 'end-in-itself', as Kant puts it, that can never legitimately be used simply as a means. Instead, he treats himself as a thing that can be used for other purposes. The would-be suicide is then, for

Kant, guilty of a lack of self-respect. Kant's conclusion appears to be that if it is not morally permissible for me to end my life under any circumstances, I have an absolute obligation to preserve my life.[1]

Kant's arguments, though ingenious, are unconvincing since it is simply not true that a person wishing to die and being willing to take her life is caught in a formal contradiction or even, for that matter, in an inconsistency. Again, it may be that, as Kant says, in some cases people commit suicide because they lack respect for themselves as persons and can no longer take responsibility for themselves. But in other cases people consider taking their lives precisely because they do have a proper self-respect and do not wish to die in circumstances where they will no longer be autonomous selves or persons in control of their lives. Biologically they will still be in existence, but as autonomous moral agents or persons they will no longer be there. It is not so much that such people wish to 'die with dignity' ('dying with dignity' is a misleading slogan since many kinds of dying are 'undignified') but rather that they wish to 'die with autonomy' since what they want is to die as autonomous human beings who are, to some degree at least, in control of their own lives.

This, in fact, provides us with a criterion for distinguishing between the cases where suicide is, as Kant argues, motivated by lack of moral respect for oneself as a person, and cases where suicide is motivated precisely by respect for oneself as an autonomous moral agent. The first is not an exercise of true autonomy, the latter is. (Even though it has prejudicial connotations, I use the term 'suicide', in what follows, in its etymological sense to refer to both kinds of deliberately ending one's life.)

Kant was, no doubt, reflecting the common Western tradition of thought which saw suicide as inspired by cowardice and weakness — a refusal to endure the difficulties and suffering of life — and also, rather ambivalently, by a kind of hubris which led people to usurp the role of God as the arbiter of life and death. The idea that since God gives us life only God can take it away runs deep in the Judaic and Christian traditions, even though it

31

sits rather inconsistently with the status given by both religious traditions to the martyr who deliberately offers up her life and dies for God. In the Middle Ages, theologians such as St Thomas Aquinas used a battery of arguments — theological, philosophical and utilitarian — to show that suicide is a sin. Thus Aquinas claims that the deliberate taking of one's life goes against our 'natural' inclination to preserve ourselves; it is a sin against charity since as a matter of charity everyone should cherish or love themselves; it is an offence against the community since every person is a part of the community and what damages each person damages the community; it is an attempt to play God since life is God's gift and God alone has the authority to decide when a person should die.[2] With respect to the last point, Aquinas admits that concerning the rest of his life a person must use his free will and make his own autonomous decisions; it is only regarding his death that he must leave the decision to God.[3] Again, Aquinas argues that suicide is not an act of true courage but rather of the 'softness of spirit' (*mollities animi*) of a person not able to bear with life's afflictions.

It must be said that much remains unclear in Aquinas' arguments against suicide. For example, if it is against the natural law to take one's life does this mean that I have an absolute duty to preserve my life at all costs and that I have a correlative duty to shun occasions where my life is endangered? Contemporary followers of Aquinas certainly do not hold that we have an absolute obligation to preserve life at all costs or that we cannot bring about our death by refusing medical treatment in certain circumstances. Again, if only God can decide when I should die how do I know what God's decision is? Say I am afflicted with some illness which if left untreated will result in my dying; should I see the illness as God's will for me and forgo any medical treatment in a spirit of fatalism? If I had medical treatment would I be defying God's decision that I should die through that illness? Would having that treatment be tantamount to 'playing God'? Or does the idea that only God can take my life simply (and vacuously) mean that when I die from 'natural causes' (and not from any deliberate act of my own) this is defined as God 'taking my life'? Certainly it is difficult to see why I cannot control the manner of my dying by my free will if, as Aquinas admits, I must control the rest of my life by my free will.

Quite apart from this, Aquinas and other Christian and Jewish theologians simply do not consider the possibility that I might in good conscience choose to 'lay down' my life or deliberately terminate it out of proper self-love, or love for others or for my country, or even out of love and respect for God.

Traditional ideas about suicide still, of course, retain some force: in many societies attempted suicide is still seen as a crime and being an accessory to suicide as equally a criminal offence. However, there has been a developing recognition, over the last thirty or forty years, of what has been called a 'right to die'. Like all such catchy slogans, the 'right to die' slogan can be misleading, but what it means is that people have the right, as autonomous moral agents, to decide in certain circumstances that their quality of life is so diminished that continued existence is humanly pointless and may therefore be ended by themselves. (The term 'euthanasia' is now so hopelessly compromised that it is better to dispense with it altogether.) Put in another way, people have the right to determine and control the circumstances of their deaths, just as they determine and control the circumstances of their lives. Dying is, in a sense, the most important thing a person does and one should as far as possible be in control of it. I do not exercise my moral autonomy by allowing my life to be dictated by chance and external forces, and neither do I exercise my moral autonomy by fatalistically allowing my death to be dictated by chance and external forces. It is not 'playing God' to seek freely to control the direction of my *life*, and it is not 'playing God' to seek freely to control the mode of my *dying*. For a Christian, God is not honoured by a person (made in the 'image' of God) abdicating her autonomy and freedom of will and passively submitting herself to 'fate'.

Richard A. McCormick has recently criticised 'physician assisted suicide' on the grounds that it is based on what he calls the 'absolutization of autonomy'. Exaggerated emphasis on personal autonomy, he claims, leads to a rejection of dependence on other people and a refusal of their compassion. I insist on dying in my way, when I choose and as I choose without being beholden to anyone else.[4] But, as has already been said, there is no reason why personal autonomy must be linked with this kind of isolationist and anti-social individualism. Autonomy does not mean that I cannot take advice from others about my life and death, or defer to others' opinions, or entrust myself to their care and compassion. It means, however, that in the last resort it is I, the autonomous agent, who has to make such decisions. I cannot abdicate or de-emphasise my personal autonomy since that would be tantamount to abdicating or de-emphasising my status as a moral agent or person. In fact, to complain of the 'absolutisation of autonomy' is rather like complaining of absolutising personhood. Autonomy is not something that one can have too much of.

This developing recognition of the right of a person freely to determine and control, so far as is possible, the mode of his or her death, has come about in various ways. First, there has been in various countries the development of medical treatment legislation which enables a competent patient, in certain situations, to refuse medical treatment and so bring about her or his death. The same legislation enables people to designate proxies to make similar decisions to refuse treatment on their behalf when they are no longer competent to make their own decisions. The legislation usually stops short of allowing a patient to ask for active intervention on the part of the physician or nurse to help bring about death. The standard rationale for this is that while I may refuse further treatment in the sure knowledge that this will bring about my death, I may not actively cause the termination of my life by direct intervention. There is, it is argued, a valid, if fine, distinction between on the one hand my request to have medical treatment withdrawn and 'letting' or 'allowing' myself to die as a consequence, and on the other hand killing myself or asking a physician or nurse to kill me. I may bring about my death by refusing any longer to be connected to a life-support system, but I may not bring about my death by giving myself a lethal injection or requesting another to give me such an injection. The former is characterised as 'letting die' and the latter as 'killing'.

There is, however, a growing scepticism about the use of the distinction between 'letting die' and 'killing' in many medical situations. In itself, of course, the distinction is a valid one and there are many cases where it applies quite legitimately. But there are also many cases where its application seems to be completely artificial, as in the cases we have been discussing here, where a person conscientiously and deliberately decides, for serious reasons, to bring about his or her death by refusing medical treatment.

Again, there has been a remarkable, if tentative and incomplete, development in recent ethical and legal thinking with regard to the medical treatment of incompetent patients, including gravely disabled newborn infants. In effect, the distinction just described, and now commonly accepted, in the case of adult competent patients (their physical or biological survival versus the point or worth or value or 'quality' of their life) has been extended to incompetent patients. This involves, as we shall see, the difficult question of how 'decisions' about life and death can be imputed to incompetent patients who cannot make those decisions for themselves.

We are here very far from Kant's (and traditional Christian and Jewish) views about the taking of one's life and the obligation to preserve one's life at all costs. In my view, as I have indicated, these developments (tentative though they are) represent a considerable progress in ethical understanding and I would like now to discuss them in some detail and to investigate how far they can be extended. In particular I am interested to analyse how a liberal society and its legislative and legal processes can cope with these developments.

A moral right to die?

A US President's Commission report on life-sustaining treatment dilates at some length on what it calls 'the disservice done by empty rhetoric' apropos of death and dying. Discussions in this area, the report complains, 'have been confused by the use of slogans and code words such as "right to die", "death with dignity" "quality of life", "euthanasia" etc., whose meanings have become hopelessly blurred'.

> In recent years many have commented on the claim that patients have a 'right to die with dignity'. Much can and should be done to ensure that patients are treated with respect and concern throughout life. Insofar as 'death with dignity' means that the wishes of dying patents are solicited and respected, it is a concept the Commission endorses. Many who use the phrase seem to go well beyond this, however, to a vision in which everyone is guaranteed a peaceful and aesthetically appealing death. This is clearly beyond reach; a fair proportion of patients are confused, nauseated, vomiting, delirious or breathless. Avoiding these distressing symptoms is not always possible; likewise, naturalness may have to be sacrificed since mechanical assistance is sometimes required to ensure comfort at the end of life. Thus, the apparent appeal of the slogan 'dignified death' often disappears before the reality of patients' needs and desires. Comparable problems arise with other slogans that are frequently heard in discussions on life-sustaining treatment.[5]

We must, therefore, scrutinise the expression 'a right to die' very closely and try to be clear about what it really means and involves. It is best to begin with the simplest and clearest situation, where a person is fully competent to make decisions about her or his life. We can then approach the more difficult situations where a person is involved who is no longer competent, because of a loss of consciousness or for some other reason, to make decisions about her or his life and death, and even more difficult still, where gravely disabled newborn infants, who have never been conscious in any sense, are concerned.

As has already been argued, we have, as moral agents, the right to control and determine the course of our own lives and to decide how we shall live (subject, of course, to our not infringing the rights of others to do the same). This is what is meant by personal autonomy. The right to autonomy or self-determination is in fact the foundation of all other human rights, since it would make no sense to speak of 'rights' at all unless we were able to decide for ourselves and be responsible for our lives. It is, indeed, so much a part of what we mean by being a human person that it seems otiose to speak of it as being a 'right' — as though it were a distinct right among other rights. (Kant in fact defines a person as one who possesses moral autonomy.) This right to moral autonomy, as we have seen, carries with it a subsidiary right to control the duration of one's life and the manner of one's dying. A person may expose herself to certain death or 'sacrifice' her life (for example to save or defend another) or refuse medical treatment in certain circumstances, while knowing that she will surely die as a consequence, or she may directly take her life when she judges that continued existence would be morally pointless because she would no longer be an autonomous agent capable of making her life humanly meaningful in any sense at all.

If I have a moral right to end my life in such a situation then I ought not to be penalised by the law for exercising that right, and I may reasonably ask another to assist me in ending my life either by not giving me certain medical treatment or by helping me to bring about my own death. (Clearly, I cannot *oblige* another to assist me since in a liberal, ethically pluralist society others may have contrary ethical views on the matter of suicide.) For that assistance, the other ought not to be penalised for acting as my servant. If it is not, in certain cases, morally wrong to end my life, it cannot be morally wrong for another to assist me in this act. As the English moral philosopher Philippa Foot argues:

> It does not seem that one would infringe someone's right to life in killing him with his permission and in fact at his request. Why should someone not be able to waive his right to life, or rather, as would be more likely to happen, to cancel some of the duties of non-

interference that this right entails? (He is more likely to say that he should be killed by this man at this time, in this manner, than to say that anyone may kill him at any time and in any way.) ... An objection might be made on the ground that only God has the right to take life but ... religion apart, there seems to be no case to be made out for an infringement of rights if a man who wishes to die is allowed to die or even be killed.[6]

My right to control, so far as is possible, the mode of my dying includes, as we have seen, my right to control the mode of my medical treatment, and this in turn dictates the nature of the relationship I have with my physician or other health professionals. Apropos the Karen Ann Quinlan case, where a completely comatose patient was kept alive by artificial means, McCormick argues that the problem there arose because it was assumed by her physicians that they 'had a right to treat the patient unasked — indeed opposed'.[7] In fact, he says,

the individual, having the prime obligation for his own health care, has also thereby the right to the necessary means for such basic health care — specifically, the right of self-determination in the acceptance or rejection of treatment. When an individual puts himself into a doctor's hands, he engages the doctor's services; he does not abdicate his right to decide his own fate.

McCormick cites a statement by Pope Pius XII in 1957 making the same point:

The rights and duties of the doctor are correlative to those of the patient. The doctor, in fact, has no separate or independent right where a patient is concerned. In general, he can take action only if the patient, explicitly or implicitly, directly or indirectly, gives him permission.[8]

One would, no doubt, need to qualify the idea that the patient–physician relationship is analogous to the master–servant relationship (where the patient is master and the physician servant) since the physician and other health carers have their own professional autonomy which has to be respected. Nevertheless, as against the old paternalistic model — physician is to patient as parent is to child — McCormick's view is on the side of the angels.

Decriminalising suicide

It follows from what has been said so far that in a liberal society, based on the principle of the moral autonomy of the individual, the law should not be concerned with preventing people from taking their lives in certain circumstances. In other words, whether suicide may or may not be a sin in some situations, it should not be a crime. It would have to be shown that suicide involved direct harm to others and was in some obvious sense an anti-social act before it could be made a crime. Of course, some argue on consequentialist grounds that even if suicide is not morally wrong in itself, its legal toleration would in effect give state endorsement and support to it and would encourage suicide among mentally disturbed people, the elderly and so on. Further, it is claimed, legal toleration of suicide would injure community respect for the 'sanctity of human life' which is central to any society and would inevitably lead to 'mercy killing' and worse. But first, the fact that the state decriminalises suicide does not imply that it endorses suicide as morally acceptable, any more than the decriminalisation of prostitution and homosexuality means that the state endorses those sexual practices as morally acceptable. What the state does, in effect, is to declare that suicide, like prostitution and homosexuality, falls within the province of personal morality and is, as such, not the law's business.

Second, it is not enough simply to argue that the decriminalisation of suicide and providing assistance to suicide may *possibly* have deleterious consequences for society as a whole. One would need to show empirically that those anti-social consequences are significantly probable or likely. The same argument from mere possibility has of course been used in the past against the decriminalisation of prostitution and homosexuality. But, as we know, society has not in fact been seriously injured by the law's toleration of them.

The recent Remmelink Commission's report on euthanasia in the Netherlands (1991) raised some questions about the effects of decriminalising assisted suicide and possible abuses of the present tolerant system in that country.[9] But it is difficult to ascertain whether the virtual decriminalisation of assisted suicide in the Netherlands has brought about a significant *increase* in the number of doctors and nurses inducing death in their patients without the latter's consent, since there is no base data about the situation that prevailed in the Netherlands before the present legislation. Again, the remedy for any abuses would appear to be more stringent controls over the determination of the actual or implied consent of patients, rather than the total prohibition of assisted suicide at the request of patients. Certainly some hospitals in the Netherlands take extreme care to ensure that patients are able to make a genuinely informed decision about requesting assistance to end their lives.[10]

Finally, it is not at all evident that a policy of preserving human life at all costs, against the wishes of patients and over-riding their autonomy, testifies to community respect for the sanctity of human life. As a French theologian, Patrick Verspieren, has argued: 'What significance does the pro-longation of biological life have if it is obtained at the cost of a serious interference with someone's liberty?'[11]

It follows from what has been said that if suicide can be moral and legal then assisting a person to commit suicide should also be moral and legal. Here, however, the state does have a right to step in to control such situations in order to ensure that the patient is capable of initiating and consenting to such an arrangement in an informed way, and is not subject to coercion either by family members or by medical staff. Thus, under the present Dutch system the law, at least in theory, controls and regulates the arrangements made between terminally ill patients and their physicians in order to ensure that such arrangements are guided by a concern for the autonomy of the individual patient. At the same time the Dutch law does not explicitly decriminalise suicide since the latter, despite efforts to reform the law, is still held to be a crime, as is assistance to suicide. This is, no doubt, a relic of older religious and cultural views about suicide and is also motivated by the mistaken (and anti-liberal) idea that if the state decriminalises suicide it thereby endorses it as being morally acceptable.

However, the Dutch law allows exceptions to the law, formally recognised by the Supreme Court, if certain conditions are fulfilled. The patient's request must be completely voluntary and persistent; he or she must be in a 'hopeless situation' or suffering from a serious illness without any hope of recovery; the physician's decision-making process must be confirmed with colleagues.[12] If those conditions are met then the physician involved will not be held to have committed a criminal offence. This situation is similar to the legal provisions governing abortion in many societies. Abortion is legally a criminal offence but under certain specified conditions (if, for example, the woman's physical or psychological health would be injured by continued pregnancy) it is not deemed to be a crime. Realistically speaking, perhaps all that can be expected at present with regard to the decriminalisation of suicide is something similar to the situation regarding abortion. In other words, while suicide and assistance to suicide remain criminal offences, exceptions will be specified as being allowed, subject to regulation and control.

Multicultural attitudes to death and dying

By way of parenthesis, it is worthwhile taking account of the 'multicultural' aspects of this question, since a liberal society tolerates and even encourages widely differing cultural attitudes and lifestyles within it. So far we have been discussing views of death and dying in what might be called the mainstream culture. But other minority groups have very different views. Traditional cultures, it has been claimed, see death 'as a distinctively social event and the dying man and those around him as fulfilling social roles'.[13] As a consequence, 'if there is a right time to die, and a time when it is not open to one to choose, then one can have no right to bring about one's death prematurely'.[14] 'Our dominant culture' the author goes on, 'lacks any coherent

41

concept, and perhaps any concept at all, of a right way to die or a wrong way to die, of a good death or a bad death'.[15]

Since our dominant culture is one based upon the liberal value of individual autonomy, it is hardly surprising that no one now recognises or accepts that there is a socially imposed and traditionally sanctioned 'right way to die' which allows no scope for choice in the way one dies. Indeed, one might say that it is not only not surprising but also not regrettable, since it marks progress in moral consciousness when one has a right to control and choose the way one dies in the same way that one controls and chooses the way one lives.

However, in a culturally pluralist society the mainstream culture must tolerate and be sensitive to minority cultures' views on death and dying as well as recognising that its own views are embedded within a complex network of cultural beliefs and attitudes and have a certain degree of cultural relativity. This does not, however, involve any kind of cultural relativism which would see the values of liberalism as being culturally determined.[16]

It is worthwhile looking briefly at the views of dying and ending one's life in the major world religious and cultural traditions. For example, the standard Jewish position is that 'only the Creator, who bestows the gift of life, may relieve man of that life, even when it becomes a burden rather than a blessing'.[17] According to the Halacha,

hastening death in order to relieve pain is not allowed, and the shortening of a dying patient's life is forbidden even if he suffers terribly. One may not be released from pain at the cost of one's life . . . The doctor has no authority to decide on lethal treatment for his critically ill patient, and he will be regarded as a murderer if he kills the patient in order to save him from further suffering. Finally, no one is entitled to ask his neighbour to kill him, as one has no power to appoint an agent for the fulfilment of something that one is not authorised to fulfil oneself.[18]

Again, according to Islamic law, God is the author of life

and, as it were, 'owns' us. Since we do not own our our lives we cannot take them.[19] (In parenthesis, there is a curious version of this argument in Plato's *Phaedo*.[20] Our lives are the property of the gods and we cannot give away what is not *our* property, unless the gods make it clear that we can.) These views are of course bound up inextricably with Jewish and Islamic religious beliefs and they are addressed principally to their own religious believers. It is difficult to see them as universal ethical prescriptions addressed to Jews and non-Jews, Muslims and non-Muslims, believers and non-believers alike. If one is a Jew or a Christian or a Muslim, one's concept of God as a creator, as a providential being with a continuing interest in his creatures, and as a unitary being, will play a major part in determining what one may or may not do with one's life. However, if one is a Hindu, a Buddhist or an Australian Aborigine, where that concept of God simply does not apply, one's attitude to taking one's life may be quite different.

These differences are brought out vividly in a recent discussion about the care of gravely impaired newborn infants in Israel, India and Japan.[21] In Israel, an observer reports, basic Jewish religious beliefs, such as 'to save one life is as if one saves the whole world', and 'life for a second is worth life for 120 years', prevent physicians from withholding treatment from newborns. The popular religious atmosphere, this observer reports, 'precludes physicians from discontinuing respiration therapy in infants with chronic lung disease: no plugs can be pulled in this society'.[22] In Indian society, Hindu religious beliefs about fate on the one hand and rebirth on the other hand have a direct effect on the treatment of disabled newborn infants. 'Quality of life' considerations play a major part in decisions about refusing or withdrawing medical treatment from these infants.

The definition of quality of life is left to the individual physician and the family. If one dies, it is destined. If a child or infant, especially

43

one who is impaired, dies, it is felt that this is predetermined and that we as mortals cannot do anything about it.

For Hindus, 'quality of life rather than the sanctity of life is a consideration because of a strong belief in rebirth'.[23] In Japan, the care of disabled newborn infants is heavily influenced by social attitudes based upon Buddhist and Confucian teaching, especially the latter's strong emphasis on law, order, authority and social status. As a result Japanese physicians play a largely paternalistic role. A common view is that parents or families, confronted with the birth of a disabled child, cannot know what the consequences for the child, or for themselves, really are and so cannot give informed consent to any decision about either treatment or the withdrawal of treatment. Again, the value of the child is seen in relationship to the family or the larger community. As it has been put by a Japanese ethicist:

> Autonomy, an important bioethical principle in the Western social context, is out of keeping with the Japanese cultural tradition. Our culture, nurtured in Buddhist and Confucian teaching, has developed the idea of suppressing the egoistic self. To be autonomous and independent is sometimes regarded as egocentric. Thus in Japan each human being is dependent on others in the family, and the social, economic and political communities.[24]

Smaller traditional societies often have views about life and death that are very different from our own. Thus, for example, the Akamba people of Kenya take the view that older males should be saved before younger males because the former usually have a larger and more complex network of relationships with others in the community and thus their death would damage more people.[25] Again, even within our own mainstream community there can be very deep differences about these matters between, for example, rural and urban people.[26]

In a liberal society which has ethnic and religious minorities within it, these different views about death and dying and whether or not we have a right to die as we choose have of course to be tolerated, and physicians and health carers must be sensitive to them in providing appropriate medical treatment. But there is no reason why, in a liberal and multicultural society, the views of certain religious groups should be in opposition to the liberal view outlined above or why members of those groups should demand that their particular view should be made into a law binding everyone. It may offend some orthodox Jews or Muslims that suicide be decriminalised in our society, just as it offends some Catholics that divorce and abortion are legally permitted. But in a liberal ethically pluralist society none of them has a right to ask the state to intervene in matters within the sphere of private morality. They may, as Mill says, remonstrate and argue with each other and the rest of society, and attempt to persuade them, but they may not invoke the law to recognise and officially endorse their view as against other views.

Choosing for those who cannot choose for themselves

The cases considered so far have been mainly about competent patients who have been able to make autonomous decisions about ending their lives or have been able to appoint proxies and give them clear instructions so that they (the proxies) can make decisions for them. The moral position in such cases is clear, though it may be far from clear in actual practice, and the position of the state and the law, at least in a liberal society, is also clear.

But the situation becomes much more complex in those cases where people are not able to make autonomous decisions for themselves, nor to designate and appoint proxies, and where someone else has to make a decision for them or where a decision has to be imputed to them. The principle of autonomy, which has governed the discussion so far, has also to be found a place here, but it is not obvious how this might be done.

Since the problem is at its most acute and most difficult with regard to decisions about disabled newborn infants, we shall focus on cases in this area. Recent surveys of paediatricians in Australia and Canada have shown that more than 95 per cent of them do not believe that 'every possible effort, including ordinary and extraordinary means, should be employed to sustain life' in seriously disabled newborn infants.[27] These attitudes are reflected in paediatric practice and it is well known that in intensive care of impaired newborn infants decisions are made not to sustain life on the ground that some newborn infants' quality of life is likely to be so minimal that further treatment is pointless.

On the other hand, until recently, the attitude of the law in most countries has been that physicians have an obligation to use all possible means to save the life of such infants. Under medical treatment legislation the law may allow competent adult patients to refuse medical treatment even though this results in the patient's death, but a monstrously disabled child has no legal right to escape or refuse life-sustaining treatment, no matter how pointless the prolongation of its life may be. There is then a notable discrepancy between medical practice in the case of newborn children and the legal situation regarding that practice. That discrepancy or gap has been closed in the case of adult competent patients with the advent of medical treatment legislation, but it remains with regard to disabled infants. As a result, the well developed medical practices used in intensive care units, which involve decisions concerning the quality of life of infants, are still not formally acknowledged by the law, and physicians and nurses run the risk of legal action being taken against them.

Recently, however, there has been a tentative development in the law which recognises that in some circumstances medical treatment may be refused or withdrawn on the ground that continued active treatment would not improve the child's 'quality of life' even if it did permit its continued physical survival. Thus, in a series of Court of Appeal cases in the UK the expected quality of a disabled infant's future life was seen as a relevant factor in making decisions about medical treatment. In one of these cases Lord Justice Templeman said that the test was 'whether the life of the child is demonstrably going to be so awful that in effect the child must be condemned to die' by withdrawing active treatment.[28] Some idea of what the Justices of the Court of Appeal consider to be a 'demonstrably awful life' is provided in a 1989 judgment affecting a baby born with severe brain damage, hydrocephalus and paralysis of arms and legs, and who was blind, deaf and completely unresponsive. In this case the Court of Appeal said that treatment should be limited to the alleviation of pain and distress of the child. The purpose of the treatment, the court said, should be to 'ease the suffering of the child rather than to achieve a short prolongation of her life'.[29] In other words, the physicians were not obliged to sustain the child's life by all possible medical means.

In a case in 1990 the Court of Appeal decided that a severely disabled pre-term child should not be given active treatment by using mechanical ventilation. In this case the court also used the quality of life criterion but in a rather different way. The question was, the Justices said, whether the child's life, from its point of view, was likely to be so intolerable if it were to continue living that it would choose to die were it in a position to make such a decision for itself. The court also said that the main consideration was what was in the baby's best interests: 'The parents owe the child a duty to give or withhold consent (to treatment) in the best interests of the child and without regard to their own interests or the interests of the community' (for example, the cost to the community of medical care).[30]

It may be noted that the notion of 'quality of life' has a number of different connotations in the Court of Appeal judgments. First, it is defined in terms of the suffering and distress to the child that prolongation of its life by active treatment would occasion. Second, it is defined in terms of what the child would choose if it were able to choose, the implication being that some forms of life are so 'awful' that no one would choose to go on living. Third, it is defined more generally in terms of the 'best interests of the child', the implication here being that it might be in the best interests of the child not to have its existence prolonged by active treatment. No doubt these three definitions overlap in practice; nevertheless they are distinct and should not be run together.

The quality of life

If then we are to develop the argument that the Court of Appeal decisions point tentatively towards, we need a clearer definition of 'quality of life'. Pragmatically it has been used to make a distinction between physical survival and properly human life. (As Aristotle remarks, we are concerned not just with living but with living well.) But it is not easy to provide a conceptual justification for the quality of life criterion. Some have suggested, rather paradoxically, that the quality of a person's life can be measured in quantitative terms — as though people could have 'more' or 'less' quality of life! Thus a newborn child without a brain, a person in a persistent vegetative state, a deeply insane person, a person suffering from a degenerative disease, and a person suffering from a terminal illness could be placed upon a graduated scale with one person having 'more' or 'less' quality of life than another.

Of course, in a sense, utilitarianism requires that states of life must be measurable in some way, that they must be able to compared with each other according to a common measure and that they must be able to be summed or aggregated (so that two people being in a certain state is twice as 'good' or 'bad' as one person being in that state). Nevertheless, there is clearly something odd about this attempt to measure the quality of human life or to do sums about human happiness. No doubt, we do, in a general way, make comparisons between different states of life (being well, being ill, being handicapped, being comatose and so on) and we do estimate that some are 'happier' or 'better' or more 'worthwhile' or 'satisfying' than others. But, unless we are utilitarians, we are not engaged in quasi-quantitative comparisons here, as though we were weighing 'amounts' of happiness or human worthiness against each other. If we attempt to compare positive states of life — such as being in love, being a creative artist, being a scientist, being a philanthropist, being a religious believer, being a political leader — we see at once how futile it is to imagine that there can be a common measure between them, enabling us to rank one 'better' or 'worse' than another and do sums about them (as though, for example, the life of one creative artist were equivalent to the lives of two politicians!).

The naive utilitarian idea that we can quantify and compare the 'quality' of human life arises from a confusion between two distinct senses of 'quality of life'. The first is what one might call the biological and medical quality of life, and the second is the moral or personal quality of life. Sometimes they go together, but often they do not and it is quite possible for someone with a 'low' degree of biological quality of life to enjoy a 'high' quality of moral or personal life. The first is measured by medical indices in terms of bodily functioning, impairment of functioning and prospects of physical survival, and we can say of a patient that her physical condition is 'poor', 'fair' or 'good'. But the second kind of quality of life cannot be measured in these terms. Medically speaking, a patient's quality of life may be poor, but morally or personally speaking the patient's quality of life may be very rich in terms of the way she has made an autonomous life for herself despite her physical handicaps. In this sense people's quality of life or human happiness depends upon what they make of the often unpromising circumstances in which they find themselves. In the *Nicomachean Ethics*[31] Aristotle says, rather oddly, that King Priam in Homer's *Iliad* cannot be accounted 'happy' because of the calamities that came upon him in his old age. In one sense this is true: King Priam is unable to live a full (*eudaimonic*) life because of the situation he is in. But in another sense Priam is morally admirable: he is a good man who bears his misfortunes with dignity and the quality of his life is much superior to that of many of his heroic Greek enemies. It is what he, as an autonomous moral agent, has done with, or how he has coped with, his misfortunes (his old age, the loss of his family, the ruin of his kingdom) that is crucial in determining his 'quality of life' as a human being.[32]

An even more dramatic case is that of Job in the Old Testament. Deprived of family, friends and possessions, and afflicted with disease, he is 'objectively' speaking in a state of profound unhappiness. No one would want to live like that. But the Old Testament writer presents Job as maintaining his trust in God and as being happy and as morally admirable nonetheless. It is Job's 'subjective' (using that misleading term for the moment) perception of his life and of what is important to it that is essential here.

Some have been afraid of using such a subjective criterion and have argued that the 'best interests' of the patient offer a more solidly objective test. But this begs the question since the best interests of the patient can be defined only by recognising his status as an autonomous moral agent and imputing decisions to him in the way discussed above. In a sense the recognition of a patient's status as an autonomous agent is as 'objective' as anything else though it is not *measurably* objective in the same sense as a medical diagnosis of a physical illness.

Of course, we cannot completely separate the two senses (medical and moral) of 'quality of life' in a hard and fast way, since in some cases a patient's biological quality of life may be such that it prevents the development of any moral or personal quality of life at all, as for example with anencephalic children or people in a persistent vegetative state. But there are cases where, as we have seen, the patient's medical condition may be close to 'demonstrably awful' and yet there remains the possibility of some kind of personal quality of life even though it may be of brief duration.

In 1971 a UK paediatrician, Dr John Lorber, proposed selection criteria for spina bifida babies which would restrict active treatment to those likely to survive without severe handicaps. Lorber's criteria related to the size and location of the spinal opening, severe paralysis and spinal deformity, severe hydrocephalus, brain damage and the like.[33] Lorber proposed that infants with one or more of the specified conditions should not receive active treatment since such infants were not likely to survive without severe handicaps. Lorber's criteria have been challenged on medical grounds but, whatever their prognostic efficacy may be, it is clear that for him the infants' quality of life was measured wholly in medical or biological terms.

When, however, we look at the criteria of 'quality of life' tentatively proposed in the UK cases considered before, a much larger definition emerges. There the crucial test is whether the continued physical survival of the child will be in its best interests in that it will allow some kind of normal development: that is, allow the child to 'make' something of its future life within the limits imposed by its severe physical handicaps. In other words, will it allow for the future exercise of moral autonomy, even if it be to a minimal degree or for a brief period? In the case of the adult competent patients discussed before, what is crucial is the perception or judgment of such patients that their lives are not worth living. In other words, the estimation of a patient's quality of life is dependent upon the patient's own decision and judgment about the purpose, meaning or value of his or her life. The worth, value or quality of my life cannot be measured 'objectively' (as my physical condition can) without reference to what I choose to do, as an autonomous moral agent, with my life. That is why any utilitarian account must be inadequate, since a person's life cannot be estimated in terms of measurable pain and suffering, or dissatisfaction outweighing or being outweighed by measurable benefits or satisfactions, but rather of whether or not some point or moral significance can possibly be given to, or made out of, the pain and suffering.

In those cases of adult patients who are no longer competent it is reasonable to impute such perception, judgment and choice to them — the test being, would they have seen any human meaning, as autonomous moral agents, if they were faced with the situation they are now in? And in the case of newborn infants, who are incapable of any perception or judgment about the human worth of their lives, the only thing we can do is to put

51

ourselves in their place and *impute* such a perception and judgment to them *as though* they were autonomous moral agents. The
test here must be: would the infant wish to lead such a life if it
had the capacity of choosing for itself? Is there a chance, however slender, of the child doing something, however minimal
and for however brief a time, with its future life despite its
physical disabilities; or are those physical disabilities so grave
that it could not possibly give any worth or value or human
meaning to its life? Willy nilly we have to make decisions for
such children and impute judgments and decisions to them.
Those who argue that the child's life must be preserved at all
costs, so that in effect the child is denied any right to refuse
treatment (a right that adult competent patients have), are also
making a decision for the child and imputing a judgment about
its future life to it, just as much as the parents and physicians
who decide to forgo active treatment for a gravely disabled
child.

A final decision about whether or not active treatment should
be given to a gravely handicapped infant cannot then be made
solely on medical grounds, as though one could judge or diagnose how much specifically human worth, value or 'quality' a
person's life had solely by 'objective' medical observations and
tests, very much in the way that one can medically diagnose
whether or not a person has AIDS or Alzheimer's disease. Such a
judgment, as we have seen, must take into account the child's
future quality of life, defined in the personal and moral terms
suggested. In other words, the right we accord to adult competent patients, as autonomous moral agents, to refuse medical
treatment they judge to be humanly pointless, should be extended to disabled newborns even though this right can only be
exercised, in their case, through a proxy acting on their behalf
and imputing a decision to them.

The liberal society and the right to die

Our discussion has shown that individual patients must (by their
own decision, through a designated proxy or by a decision

imputed to them) make a final decision about the ending of their own lives, rather than a physician or some other external agent making a decision on the basis of some supposedly 'objective' medical evidence about the degree of value or quality of a patient's life, or on the basis that the prolongation of a patient's life would be a social and economic burden.

Some have seen the admission of a right to die as the first step on a slippery slope that will end inevitably in something like the Nazi euthanasia program in the 1930s, when some 275 000 people were judged on objective 'scientific' grounds to be 'socially useless' and then killed by medically qualified staff in hospitals and sanatoriums. Medical staff were not expressly ordered to kill these inmates but were simply given permission to do so. These centres were the prototypes of the later extermination camps for the Jews and other 'racially inferior' peoples.[34] But a 'right to die' which is grounded at all levels on the moral autonomy of the individual is totally at odds with that position. We are on a slippery slope only when we move away from seeing the decision to end one's life as a moral decision belonging to the individual patient, and as being grounded in the patient's right to moral autonomy, to seeing it as primarily a medical or scientific matter, or as a social matter (taking into account, for example, whether the prolonged life of a handicapped newborn infant would be a burden upon its parents or on society at large). In a liberal society then, any legislation giving expression to a 'right to die' must relate essentially to the patient's autonomous right to control the ending of her or his life. Extraneous considerations, for example whether the continuation of a patient's life is a burden on parents, family or society in general, should not be taken into account.

Legislation must make it clear that it is the patient, or the patient's proxies, who make the decision (though of course with the benefit of medical advice) to terminate his or her life, not the physicians or the agents of medical institutions. There is a fine but important line between the patient making his or her own decision using the advice of physicians and other health professionals, and the physicians making the decision while taking into account the patient's wishes. From this point of view, the following statement by a group of eminent American physicians places the emphasis in exactly the wrong place: thus, after acknowledging that 'the patient's role in decision-making is paramount', the group then goes on to say that 'the patient's right to accept or refuse treatment notwithstanding, the physician has a major role in the decision-making process. He or she has the knowledge, skills and judgment to provide diagnosis and prognosis, to offer treatment choices and explain their implications, and to assume responsibility for recommending a decision with respect to treatment'.[35]

From this point of view, an American medical ethicist, Robert Weir, has made some useful suggestions about decision-making procedures which would help to safeguard and promote the interests of the patient rather than the interests of the parents, the family, the physicians, the hospital or the community at large.[36] Weir is mainly concerned with decisions about handicapped newborn children, but what he says also applies to decision-making apropos of other patients. After detailing criteria which proxy decision-makers should satisfy — they should have relevant information and knowledge, be impartial, not be under severe emotional stress, and be consistent — he argues that, although parents of newborns should of course play a major part in proxy decisions, they have only a *prima facie* right to make decisions for their child. As he says: 'All parents simply do not promote the best interests of the birth-defective children born to them. In fact, it is a false assumption to think that all parents in these circumstances have the capacity to be either altruistic or impartial toward the handicapped newborns in their families'.[37]

The physician has also, according to Weir, a right to play a part in the decision-making process, but the physician's contribution, along with the views of the parents and other proxies, ought to be considered finally by a special committee comprising a physician and a nurse, a patient advocate, a parent advocate, an ethicist, a social worker and a lawyer.[38] If need be, the committee could appeal to a court of law, although this should be a rare occurrence. Weir goes on to specify three safeguards that should accompany any decision in favour of non-treatment of a patient: '(a) the proxies in a case should consult with appropriate medical specialists and other professionals before making a decision to deny treatment; (b) the decision should not be carried out for a set period of time (perhaps a week) to allow for greater emotional stability by the parents and the possibility of a custody hearing, should they be warranted; (c) the attending physician should provide written reasons concerning why the diagnostic condition was not treated, or why treatment in this case was judged to be optional'.[39] In effect, in Weir's scheme, the parents, physicians and committee would constitute a kind of collective proxy.

Although these provisions may appear to be unduly elaborate and cumbersome, something like them is necessary if the ending of a patient's life, whether competent to choose or not, is to be seen as an expression of the patient's autonomous right to die. In a liberal society that latter consideration must be paramount. No doubt, with some ethnic groups the family has a very large part in making decisions about death and dying (as they do about marriage and other matters). But the family decision cannot, finally, overrule the decision of the individual. It would be unthinkable in a liberal society for medical treatment to be removed because of a family decision when that is against the express wishes of the patient. Though there may be difficulties in reconciling liberal values with different cultural approaches to death and dying, and while a great of sensitivity is needed in negotiating those difficulties, the liberal society cannot abdicate its central commitment to the value of personal autonomy.

Death and the hospital

By way of an addendum to the discussion above it is of interest to look at the institution of the hospital, since many of the problems we have been considering about death and dying arise from the fact that the majority of people now die in hospitals which are centres of sophisticated medical technology. An American report notes that something like 80 per cent of deaths in the US take place in hospitals and long-term care institutions,[40] and these institutions use medical technology which enables life to be sustained and prolonged far beyond what 'nature', would allow in an extra-institutional context. This is particularly true of pre-term handicapped infants and, at the other end of the spectrum, elderly people (who are claimed to be the major consumers of medical technology). This is not to suggest, in a Luddite way, that medical technology is evil and that we should return to letting pre-technological nature take its course with the lives of handicapped children and elderly people (though it has been suggested that there is a natural span of life beyond which people should not receive treatment by expensive medical technology).

All socio-cultural structures have a cost–benefit aspect in that they disclose certain possibilities and allow certain things to be done, but at the same time close off other possibilities and prevent other things being done. This is true also of the large, modern and high-technology hospital. It has immense benefits but it also exacts considerable costs. It allows a certain style of medicine to be practised and certain patient–health-carer relationships to obtain, but it also inhibits other styles of medical treatment and of patient–health-carer relationships.

It would be interesting to investigate the emergence of the institution of the hospital as a cultural phenomenon. As we know, a great many cultures have elaborate systems of health care but nothing at all like the hospital.[41] In fact, the hospital as we know it is a recent arrival within our own culture, being no more than 150 years old. If we looked at the emergence of the hospital with the eye of an anthropologist we would see it as an historically contingent phenomenon appearing at a particular time in Western culture in response to a complex set of socio-cultural factors: not just as the institutional expression of the 'scientific medicine' that became established in the nineteenth century but also as the expression of the movement within European culture towards what the French thinker Michel Foucault calls *renfermement* or 'enclosure'. For Foucault the emergence of the hospital is linked with the emergence of the asylum, the factory, the modern prison, the school, even the modern family — all forms of institutional 'enclosure' which he connects with the increase of state 'surveillance' and control from the eighteenth century onwards.[42]

Again, the hospital can be seen as the institutional expression of the mechanistic spirit that pervaded science and medicine in the eighteenth and nineteenth centuries. The US medical sociologist, Elliot Mishler, for example, has claimed that the introduction of the machine model into medicine, the professionalisation of medicine and the coming into being of the hospital all went hand in hand. As he says, ' a machine model of the body is central to the way the profession of medicine entered the twentieth century'.[43]

Mishler also notes that the Flexner Report (1910) redefined the nature of medicine in terms of technology:

> Medical curricula and practice were shaped around what was easily standardised and defined in technological models. To work appropriately and to claim expertise in the late nineteenth and early twentieth centuries was to work with standardised objects defined in isolation from their social context. The body became a standardised object, and the medical curriculum organised around standardisable skills.[44]

As a result death was transformed from a human and religious phenomenon into 'a problem of bodily function'. 'Attention was directed to the body and — as with so many aspects of nature — it became a machine susceptible to repair and intervention'.[45] From this redefinition of health, illness and death, and from the professionalisation of health carers that it led to, the institution of the hospital as we know it developed. At all events, whatever its historical and socio-cultural origins, the hospital is now in our society the principal context within which health care is provided, and within which death takes place, just as in our society the school is the principal context within which education is provided.

As an institution the modern, large-scale, high technology hospital is inevitably 'bureaucratic' (in the non-pejorative Weberian sense): in other words, it necessarily has formalised, impersonal procedures and routines to ensure the efficient functioning of the institution; and the spontaneous and personal or 'charismatic' element (once again in the Weberian sense) is correspondingly diminished. One cannot run a large and complex institution on spontaneous 'charismatic' impulses. Again, with such a structure a hierarchy of roles is set up with complex relations of power between the various roles (patient, family of patient, nurses, doctors, paramedics, administrators, general staff) so that institutional 'politics' becomes inevitable and important. In this context there is a strong tendency towards bureaucratic paternalism and a real danger that the autonomy of the patient will be devalued.

An analogy might be made here with the institution of the school and the professionalisation of the teaching role. Thus the teacher who starts out as an instructor in certain skills and in the provision of access to a body of knowledge, tends to take over the role of parent, to become a kind of social worker and psychiatrist, even to become a kind of priest or (as Jacques Barzun once put it) a 'soul carer'. The teacher and the school become indispensable, since without the certification provided by the school the student is not officially 'educated'. The rhetoric of course is that the student is the primary agent in education and that the teacher and the school have the modest ancillary role of aiding or enabling the student to achieve autonomy as a learner: but in reality the teacher and the school, as we know, are given more and more paternalistic power by society, and other agencies of education — the family, the peer group, the community and subcommunities — are correspondingly devalued.

Much the same thing happens with the institution of the hospital vis-à-vis heath care. The physician and other health carers are supposed to be the ancillaries or servants of the patient. According to the ancient definition of medicine it is an art that co-operates with nature (in this case the human body) and enables (not causes) the body to restore itself to health. However, the hospital institution leads health carers gradually to assume the role of primary agents or causes of the patient's health.

One must, of course, be realistic about what is and is not possible in the institutional context of the large, high technology hospital and one must also recognise (as against critics like Ivan Illich) the enormous gains and benefits in health care for which such hospitals have been responsible. However, a good deal could be done to restructure the system to alleviate the bureaucatic and technological impersonality and paternalism of the hospital and to make it more responsive to patients' needs and more respectful of patient autonomy. Again, extra-hospital health-care contexts should be built up to provide genuine choices for patients. The hospice movement for the care of the terminally ill is a good example of what might be done here. As a US observer has argued:

With health care becoming more bureaucratised, there are limits to what can be achieved at the doctor–patient level in structure, content and process. Increasingly medical care is being determined not by individual physicians but by large institutions that employ or reimburse them. If physicians are helpless against such agencies, patients are doubly so. It will take larger changes in state and federal laws and financing mechanisms governing health care to restructure the system in ways that will benefit all patients, not just those with enough money, persistence and savvy to work the system. Without such reforms, health care will remain inefficient and inequitable, and patients' efforts to transform the doctor–patient relationship will have only limited impact.[46]

All this is especially relevant to the question of making the hospital, and the health-care system generally, sensitive to the autonomy of the individual patient, particularly in the delicate but momentous area of patients making decisions about the manner of their dying. Here, more than in any other sphere of medicine, physicians must see themselves, while maintaining their own professional autonomy and recognising their own professional obligations, as the ancillaries of the patient, whether the patient is competent or incompetent.

NOTES

1. Immanuel Kant, *Foundation of the Metaphysics of Morals*, 1785, trans. Carl J. Friedrich, in *The Philosophy of Kant*, New York, Modern Library, 1949.
2. *Summa Theologiae*, 2a, 2ae, q.64, art. 5.
3. See 2a, 2ae, q.65, art. 5 ad 3.
4. Richard A. McCormick, 'Physician assisted suicide: flight from compassion', *Christian Century*, 108, 1991, p.1132.
5. *Deciding to Forgo Life-Sustaining Treatment: A Report on the Ethical, Medical, and Legal Issues in Treatment Decisions*, President's Commission for the Study of Ethical Problems in Medicine and Biomedical and Behavioral Research, Washington, US Government Printing Office, 1983.
6. Philippa Foot, 'Euthanasia', in Ernan McMullin ed., *Death and Decision*, Washington, American Association for the Advancement of Science, Selected Symposium 18, 1978, pp.102-3.
7. Richard A. McCormick, 'Legislation and the Living Will', in the same author's *How Brave a New World?*, New York, Doubleday, 1981, p.406.
8. ibid., p.406.
9. For an overview of the report, see Paul J. van der Maas *et al.*, 'Euthanasia and other medical decisions concerning the end of life', *The Lancet*, 8338, 1991, 609-74.
10. See Pieter Admiraal, 'Is there a place for euthanasia?', *Bioethics News*, Monash University, 10, 4, 1991, pp.10-22.
11. Patrick Verspieren, *Face à celui qui meurt*, Paris, Desclée de Brouwer, 1984, p.23.

12. See Maurice A. de Wachter, 'Active euthanasia in the Netherlands', *Journal of the American Medical Association*, 262, 1989, pp.3316-19.
13. Alasdair McIntyre, 'The right to die garrulously', in Ernan McMullin ed., *Death and Decision*, op. cit., p.78.
14. ibid., p.80.
15. ibid.
16. See Phillippe Ariès, *Western Attitudes Towards Death*, Baltimore, Johns Hopkins Press, 1974, and Robert Herz, 'The collective representation of death', in *Death and the Right Hand*, London, Cohen and West, 1960. On Australian Aboriginal attitudes to death see Max Charlesworth, Howard Morphy, Diane Bell, Kenneth Maddock (eds.), *Religion in Aboriginal Australia*, St Lucia, Queensland University Press, 1984, Part 2.
17. Fred Rosner, *Modern Medicine and Jewish Ethics*, New York, Yeshiva University Press, 1986, pp.142-56
18. A. Carmi, 'Live like a king: die like a king', in A. Carmi ed., *Euthanasia*, Berlin, Springer Verlag, 1984, pp.11-12.
19. See Fazlur Rahman, *Health and Medicine in the Islamic Tradition*, New York, Crossroads, 1987, p.126.
20. *Phaedo*, 61C-62D.
21. *Hastings Center Report*, August 1986, 'Caring for newborns: three world views', pp.18-23.
22. Arthur I. Eidelman, 'In Israel, families look to two messengers of God', ibid., p.19.
23. K.N. Siva Subramanian, 'In India, Nepal and Sri Lanka, quality of life weighs heavily', ibid., p21.
24. Rihito Kimura, 'In Japan parents participate but doctors decide', ibid., pp.22-3.
25. See J. Kilner, *Who Lives? Who Dies? Ethical Criteria in Patient Selection*, New Haven, Yale University Press, 1990.
26. See Nancy S. Jecker and Alfred O. Berg, 'Allocating medical resources in rural America: alternative perceptions of justice', *Soc. Sci. Med.*, 24, 1992, pp.467-74.
27. See Peter Singer, Helga Kuhse, Cora Singer, 'The treatment of newborn infants with major handicaps: a survey of obstetricians' and paediatricians' attitudes regarding the treatment of defective newborns', *Bioethics*, 5, 1991, pp.139-49.
28. Templeman L.J. in *Re B (a minor) (wardship: medical treatment)* (1981)[1990] 3 All E.R. 927, at 929. I am indebted to the paper by Loane Skene, 'Legal issues in treating critically ill newborn infants', Law Reform Commission of Victoria, 1991, for details of these cases.

29. *Re C (a minor) (wardship: medical treatment)* [1989] 2 All E.R. 782.
30. *Re J (a minor) (wardship: medical treatment)* [1990] All E.R. 930.
31. *Nicomachean Ethics* 1100a5–10.
32. See Max Charlesworth, *The Ethics of Happiness*, Geelong, Deakin University Press, 1991, p.80.
33. Cited in 'Selection in Spina Bifida', *Medical Journal of Australia*, 2, 1971, pp.1151–2.
34. See Robert Proctor, *Racial Hygiene: Medicine Under the Nazis*, Cambridge, Mass., Harvard University Press, 1989.
35. Sidney H. Wanzer *et al.*, 'The Physician's Responsibility Toward Hopelessly Ill Patients', *New England Journal of Medicine*, 310, 1988, p.956.
36. Robert Weir, *Selective Treatment of Handicapped Newborns*, New York, Oxford University Press, 1984. See especially chapter 9.
37. ibid., p.259.
38. ibid., p.272.
39. ibid.
40. *Deciding to Forgo Life-Sustaining Treatment*, op. cit., p.17.
41. See, for example, Arthur Kleinman, *Patients and Healers in the Context of Culture*, Berkeley, University of California Press, 1980; see also Catherine Berndt, 'Sickness and health in Western Arnhem Land: a traditional perspective', in Janice Reid (ed.) *Body, Land and Spirit*, St Lucia, University of Queensland Press, 1983, pp.121–38.
42. Michel Foucault, *Punir et surveiller*, Paris, Presses universitaires de France, 1975.
43. Elliot G. Mishler *et al.* (eds.) *Social Contexts of Health, Illness and Patient Care*, Cambridge, Cambridge University Press, 1981.
44. ibid., p.232.
45. ibid., p.239.
46. Dianna Dutton, 'Patient knows best, a review of Laurence C. Horowitz, *Taking Charge of Your Medical Fate*', in *The New York Times Book Review*, October 16, 1988, p.34.

4

Beginning Life

New ways of birth and family formation

Over the last thirty years there has been a profound shift in attitudes in societies in the Western European tradition towards marriage and the family, or rather to traditional means of family formation. This was set in train by 'the change from pre-arranged marriages being the norm, to the general convention that the married should choose one another',[1] and this in turn was seen as a development in personal autonomy in family relationships. Of course, the great majority of children are born from, and most families are created by, heterosexual couples in formally married unions. Again, marriage and traditional family formation are still given powerful support by the law and by the public rhetoric of our society. Further, a number of alternative ways of family formation (for example, artificial insemination by donor and *in vitro* fertilisation) are used only by people who are infertile. In this sense donor insemination and *in vitro* fertilisation (IVF) are not preferred choices but choices of last resort.

Nevertheless, there is at the same time an acceptance — sometimes passive, sometimes more positive — in our society of alternative means of procreation and of family formation, even though some of these modes of having a family (for example, homosexual couples having children by means of artificial insemination) are still seen as being questionable, and even though many people adopt quite contradictory attitudes to them (for example, most people now accept single parent families and having children through artificial insemination by donor, but many still reject surrogate motherhood as a means of family formation).

The following is a summary list of possible modes of family formation:

- Children born from heterosexual couples in formal married unions.
- Children born from heterosexual couples in stable *de facto* unions.
- Children born from a previous marriage or *de facto* union but either (a) now in a single parent situation, or (b) in a reincorporated family after divorce and remarriage so that the children have 'new' fathers or mothers.
- Children born in a single parent situation.
- Children adopted into another family (a) through 'traditional' adoption where the relinquishing mother has no contact with the child given up for adoption and the child has no access to information about its origins; (b) through 'open' adoption where the relinquishing mother can maintain contact with the child and the child can have access to information about its origins; (c) through a form of adoption where the relinquishing mother plays a part in the selection of the adoptive parents.
- Children born to heterosexual couples from artificial insemination by donor.
- Children born to homosexual (lesbian) couples from artificial insemination by donor.
- Children born from the gametes of a couple through IVF and embryo transfer.
- Children born from the gametes of donors, or donor embryos, through IVF and embryo transfer.

- Children born from surrogacy arrangements either (a) of the traditional kind where the social and biological mother contributes the ovum but cedes her role as social mother to another woman on the birth of the child, or (b) where the eventual social mother and father both contribute the gametes and the embryo is formed by IVF and then transferred to another woman who gestates it and then surrenders the child to its 'genetic' parents.

The social toleration and acceptance of most of these alternative means of procreation and family formation, and in some cases their legal endorsement, has led some to speak of a 'right to procreative liberty'.[2] In an essay engagingly entitled 'Providing protection for collaborative non-coital reproduction', an American legal scholar, Lisa C. Ikemoto, has this to say:

> Noncoital, collaborative procreation presents a greater set of choices than reproduction through sexual intercourse giving the participants the opportunity to determine the source of genetic material, the method and timing of conception, the individual who will bear the child and the persons who will raise the child. Availability of the expanded set of choices invests individuals with greater control over their genetic, biological and psychosocial destiny and hence greater autonomy. The [US] Constitution must protect decisional autonomy in procreation because our concept of liberty requires that the government leave individuals free to determine issues so core to personhood.[3]

Put in rather less radical terms, there is now a growing awareness that in a liberal society people should as far as possible be free to choose the way in which they wish to have children and the kind or style of family they wish to constitute, and they should not be penalised (for example, by being denied access to public health care funds and resources) for choosing alternatives to traditional (heterosexual and monogamous) family formation unless these latter involve some clear and serious danger to society or to the children born from such alternative modes of procreation (for example, from incestuous relationships). It is worth remarking that in Canada a physician's refusal to provide donor insemination to a single woman has been held to be an act of illegal discrimination. Again, some legal authorities in Australia have argued that the exclusion of unmarried couples and even homosexual couples from access to publicly funded reproductive technology programs runs counter to anti-discrimination legislation in that country.[4]

The different modes of family formation mentioned are now, with the exception of surrogate motherhood, accepted or tolerated in most liberal societies. No one calls for the prohibition of donor insemination, or of IVF, or of single parent families, whatever they may think about them on moral grounds. Even though perhaps most people would look askance at homosexual families, they recognise that it is practically impossible to prevent female homosexual couples from having children through donor insemination. From one point of view this is an inevitable consequence of living in a liberal democratic society where a plurality of what John Stuart Mill calls 'experiments in living' is tolerated. So long as any mode of family formation does not do obvious and direct harm to others (primarily of course to the children born of such arrangements but also to the women involved) and provided that the right of the child to information about the circumstances of its procreation is safeguarded, then it should not be prohibited by the law.

In parenthesis, it might be argued that infertility is, properly speaking, a pathological condition that affects only heterosexual couples. A homosexual couple cannot be said to be 'infertile' in any meaningful sense and, from this point of view, cannot claim access to publicly funded modes of assisted procreation or reproductive technology such as IVF, since the latter are supposed to be a treatment for infertility. However, unless one arbitrarily defines 'infertility' in terms of heterosexual pathology, there is no reason why it should not be used to describe the situation of a homosexual couple who wish to have a child and form a family. Such a couple could be described as being 'situationally infertile'. To many people, no doubt, this will seem as bizarre as speaking of a homosexual 'marriage', but the fact remains that some homosexual couples do have children and establish families.

In a celebrated surrogacy arrangement in Victoria, Australia,[5] the sister who acted as the surrogate mother was in fact fertile (she had borne three children of her own) but her husband had had a vasectomy and she was deemed by the Victorian legal authorities to be 'socially infertile' and so able to participate in an IVF program which, under Victorian legislation, is restricted to infertile women. The authorities thus extended the notion of infertility to describe the condition of a woman who, though she was in one sense fertile herself, could not, because of her married situation, have a child of her own and create a family.

Again, in a recent Australian report, *Access to Reproductive Technology*, by the former National Bioethics Consultative Committee, the breadth of the concept of 'infertility' is emphasised:

> Even the question of who is infertile is a matter of judgment. Is a fertile woman whose partner has had a vasectomy 'infertile' in the sense that she is in an infertile situation? Is a couple who have four children, two each from their previous marriages, who cannot now conceive a child together, 'infertile'? Is their inability to conceive another child judged to be the same as that of a woman with no children who has experienced a decade of unsuccessful treatment for blocked tubes? Is a fertile woman for whom pregnancy is a risk to her health, perhaps her life, 'infertile'?[6]

But what of the ethics of these various modes of family formation? A Christian will believe that the mode of monogamous, heterosexual and quasi-permanent marriage and family creation has potentialities for a special human richness and happiness. In the Christian scheme such a marriage and family life is a 'sacrament': that is, a means of God's grace. (At the same time, it has to be acknowledged that the concept of Christian marriage and family life has undergone radical changes throughout its long history.) But it certainly does not follow from the fact that one believes that Christian marriage and family formation has a special character that one has to view other modes of family formation as being morally deviant in some way or as subverting the institution of 'the family'. It may be that there are likely to be difficulties, both for parents and for children, in some alternative forms of family life and that they are likely to be less humanly rewarding. There is, of course, some evidence that children who have been adopted, and children in single or divided parent families after divorce suffer some untoward effects. But then some heterosexual and monogamous marriage-based families also have their own peculiar difficulties both for parents and for children. So far as contributing to the sum of human happiness is concerned, the traditional family has (as Freud and others have reminded us) an ambivalent and dubious record. We tend to view the traditional family in an idealised way and to conveniently forget its potentialities for personal and social harm while dwelling upon the failures, difficulties and potentialities for harm of alternative modes of family life. In general, it can be said,

> There is no simple answer to the question of how artificial means of reproduction affect our understanding of the family . . . Since there is no single, univocal concept of the family, it is a matter of moral and social decision just what determinants of 'family' should be given priority.[7]

Some have also claimed that alternative modes of family formation will necessarily have such bad effects upon the children brought into being that it would be better were they not brought into existence at all. As we shall see, this argument has been used especially against surrogate motherhood. But apart from the paradoxical nature of this argument — that the 'best interests of the child' dictate that the child be not born at all! — there is no conclusive empirical evidence that surrogacy or other modes of family formation would necessarily have such massively deleterious effects on the children involved that they should be legally prohibited. Once again, we all know the effects on children of marriage and family breakup, but no one sees this as a reason for prohibiting divorce on the ground that it is against the 'best interests of the child'.

We cannot then in a liberal society set up the traditional mode of family formation as a paragon and see all other alternative modes of family creation as deviant and subversive. Instead, while the traditional family will probably continue to be central, we have to see the concept of 'the family' as a pluralistic one and to recognise that different forms of the family can co-exist in our society. At the same time, of course, we can accept that particular groups — Christians or others — may very well think, on religious or other grounds, that certain specific modes of family formation are morally superior to others.

Bearing a child for another

In our society the practice of so-called surrogate motherhood, bearing a child for another woman, is quite unusual and out of the ordinary; it is concerned with perhaps the most sensitive area of human life, reproduction, and there have been a number of well-publicised cases — for example, Baby M, Baby Cotton — where both the surrogate mothers and the children born of surrogacy arrangements appear to have been exploited. As a consequence the very idea of surrogate motherhood stirs up powerful emotions in most people. However, ethics is a rational discipline; that is, it consists in trying to find reasons for what we think is morally good or bad. Emotional reactions or gut feelings can be important in ethics but in the last resort it is the reasons we can adduce to support our moral stances that are conclusive. Even Christians and other religious believers have to put forward reasoned arguments if they are to convince other people in the community: they cannot rest content merely with saying 'The Church forbids such and such', or 'The Bible says that so and so is wrong', or 'The Pope has declared that this or that is immoral'. (This is expressly recognised within the Roman Catholic Church, where it is claimed that the moral principles governing human sexuality and reproduction are based on the 'natural law', i.e. a

69

body of principles derived from the structure of our human nature, which are able to be known and recognised by everyone whether or not they are Catholics or Christian believers.)

When, however, one looks at the reasons put forward by those who oppose surrogacy it is hard not to find them remarkably unconvincing. Some of the arguments claim that surrogate motherhood offends against certain basic moral principles (for example, that human beings should not be used as a means to other people's ends), but they use those principles in a selective and inconsistent way. For example, a recent statement by the Australian Catholic bishops (based upon the Vatican's Congregation for the Doctrine of the Faith document *Instruction on Respect for Human Life*, 1987) argues that surrogate motherhood 'offends the dignity of the child and is contrary to the child's right to have been conceived, brought into the world and brought up by his or her parents'. The bishops here appear to be invoking a moral principle that a child has a right to expect, and society has a correlative obligation to ensure, that its social parents (the parents who are bringing it up) will be the same as its biological or genetic parents (the parents who provide the gametes for its conception). But if this is a universal moral principle, and if the bishops are to be consistent, then adoption and artificial insemination should also both be prohibited, as well as family reconstitution after divorce and remarriage. You cannot use the principle selectively to reject surrogacy and then refuse to use it with regard to adoption and artificial insemination.

This kind of selective use of principles is widespread in the anti-surrogacy arguments. Thus, as we shall see, the principle that the interests of the child must be considered to be paramount is often used against surrogacy, but then it is not used consistently in other areas. The interests of the child are, for example, not taken into account in initiating divorce and marriage break-up: it is only after the break-up that the interests of the child are considered, when determining which parent will have custody of the child. If it is a universal moral principle that the interests of the child must, in appropriate situations, be paramount then we ought, if we are to be consistent, prohibit divorce. Again, some feminists use a 'pro choice' principle (a woman has a right to use her own body as she chooses) to argue that women have a right to abortion, but they then claim that this same principle cannot be used in the case of surrogacy. In other words, they claim that the surrogate mother cannot argue that she has a right to use her body as she chooses in choosing to bear a child for another woman.

We have been referring so far to arguments of principle against surrogate motherhood. But other arguments are consequentialist in style: in other words they claim that the consequences of the practice of surrogate motherhood make it immoral — for example, that surrogate motherhood will involve the exploitation of economically and socially deprived women, or will have grave psychological effects on the children born of surrogacy arrangements, or will subvert the basic institutions of marriage and the family. However, if you are arguing that surrogate motherhood is likely in most cases to bring about large-scale deleterious consequences of this kind then you must produce actual empirical evidence to show this. You cannot just say it is *possible* that the practice of surrogacy might produce deleterious consequences for all those concerned in surrogacy arrangements. It is, after all, possible that having children in ordinary marriage and family situations might produce bad consequences for both parents and children. (As we know from the high incidence of marriage and family break-up in our society, and the consequent trauma for both partners and children, this is more than a possibility.) But this is, by itself, no argument against ordinary marriage and family formation.

However, many of the consequentialist arguments against surrogacy are of this kind: for the most part they rely on speculations about the possible consequences of surrogacy and they produce very little hard evidence to show that the practice of surrogacy actually has those consequences. Anecdotal evidence, on both sides, of course abounds and it has its own value; but if we are to make social policy decisions about surrogacy, we need scientifically controlled evidence. As a recent article in the *American Journal of Obstetrics and Gynecology* puts it:

> Although surrogate parenting programs have been in existence in the United States for a decade, published research on maternal-child health outcomes of this practice has been non-existent. This information is necessary for health care professionals and childless couples to assess the place for surrogate pregnancy in infertility care, as well as to broaden the spectrum of informed consent for the potential surrogate mother. Such data are also important for social policy decisions regarding the nature and degree of medicolegal regulation or prohibition advisable for the practice of surrogate parenting.[8]

The two styles of argument against surrogacy just described, the one based upon moral principles and the other based upon consequences, are very different and they should not be confused. If you appeal to a moral principle you are saying in effect that, regardless of the consequences, such and such an activity is right or wrong. If, on the other hand, you are using a consequentialist argument, consequences are of course all important. However, in much of the case against surrogate motherhood, the two kinds of argument are mixed up together in a completely confused way. When one points out that the anti-surrogacy proponent is using moral principles selectively and inconsistently, an appeal is then made to the supposed deleterious consequences of surrogate motherhood. On the other hand, when one points out that the consequences of surrogacy seem *prima facie* to be no worse than the consequences of ordinary family formation; the anti-surrogacy proponent then refers to principles of the kind mentioned before.

The moral of all this is that, in considering the morality of surrogate motherhood where a woman chooses to bear a child for another, it is no use relying upon gut feelings or emotion, or appealing to some kind of authority. If you are going to appeal to principles then you must be consistent in your use of those principles; if you are going to appeal to consequences you must be prepared to produce hard evidence and not just remain content with imagining mere possibilities.

Questions about surrogacy

Three main questions about surrogate motherhood need to be considered. First, is the practice of surrogate motherhood immoral in itself: in other words, does it offend against some moral principle so that, regardless of its possible consequences, it is intrinsically immoral? Most of us would hold that directly killing an innocent human being is morally wrong in itself because it offends against the ethical principle that human life has a special value. In the same way those who argue that the practice of surrogate motherhood is intrinsically immoral claim that it offends against the moral principle that one person cannot be used as a means for the purposes of another person. In commercial or contractual surrogacy (where one woman contracts for a consideration to bear a child for another), so it is argued, a woman sells herself (or her gestatory functions) to another. But even in altruistic surrogacy, it is claimed, the surrogate mother becomes an instrument or a means for the social mother's end of having a child.

The second question is this: even if it cannot be shown that surrogate motherhood is intrinsically immoral in that it flouts some basic moral principle, are the likely consequences of allowing surrogacy so deleterious that it should be prohibited? Many people in our society hold that, while taking hard drugs is not immoral in itself, and while it may be possible for some people to use hard drugs moderately, allowing free access to such drugs would have such devastating consequences that they should be banned, and users and suppliers severely punished. (We have to neglect, for the moment, the blatant inconsistency in people's attitudes here: it is well known that alcohol and tobacco have much worse consequences on people's health and on our social welfare services than hard drugs, but we give public honours to the makers of alcohol and tobacco, while putting suppliers of hard drugs in jail, and in some countries, even executing them!) In the same way, the issue here is whether allowing the practice of surrogate motherhood would have such devastating consequences that it should be banned or severely discouraged by penalising those involved.

The third issue is concerned with the relationship between personal morality and the law. Some things may be immoral and yet we do not think that there should be laws forbidding those things, since (a) it would be impracticable to enforce those laws effectively, and (b) it would bring about more harm than good to seek to enforce them. For example, many people think that adultery is morally wrong but also that it would be futile and counterproductive to have laws prohibiting adultery since it would involve a gross invasion of people's privacy to seek to enforce such laws. Many also take this view of prostitution and abortion: these practices, it is thought, are morally undesirable in themselves but any attempt to prohibit them by law would be ineffective and would probably lead to worse evils. We cannot assume then that if surrogacy were shown to be morally undesirable it should therefore be prohibited by law.

The most important consideration, however, is this: in a liberal democratic and pluralist society where people have very different moral views and attitudes, and where primary value is attached to personal freedom and self-determination or 'autonomy', there is a presumption that a woman should have the right to choose whether or not she wishes to bear a child for another. In a liberal society people should as far as possible be allowed to make their own moral decisions for themselves and it is not the business of the law to enforce a common code of morality. The law should be brought in, so to speak, only when other people are likely to be harmed in some obvious way. In the past, homosexuality was legally prohibited because many people saw it as being subversive of the fundamental sexual relationships that the family and society as a whole depend upon. Now, however, homosexuality has been decriminalised in many societies on the ground that it is concerned with an area of personal morality which is not the law's business. The issue we are considering here is, then, whether the practice of surrogacy, and the particular mode of family formation it makes possible, falls into the area of personal morality which is not the law's business. Or, put in another way, in a society where personal liberty is maximised, and where people have very different views about, and attitudes towards, sexual morality and also to family formation, why should surrogacy be prohibited by law? Most people will favour a stable heterosexual union as the basis for having children and forming a family, but others may choose to be single parents, or to use donor insemination (it has been estimated that some 5000–6000 donor inseminations are carried out each year in Australia),[9] or ivf involving donor gametes (some 12 per cent of ivf pregnancies in Australia and New Zealand in 1988 used donor oocytes, donor sperm or donor embryos). Or again, others may choose to reconstitute a family after divorce and remarriage. Given these various modes of family formation, which are accepted in our society, why should we single out surrogate motherhood for special attention and subject it to legal prohibition?

Let us then look briefly at the various issues outlined above, remembering, as I have said, that we are engaged in a rational analysis and not just an exchange of gut-feelings or a swapping of anecdotes. First, is surrogate motherhood morally wrong in itself in that it offends against some kind of moral principle? Consider the case of a woman who wishes to help another woman, a sister or a friend who cannot bear a child, by bearing the child for her. She carefully considers her action and its likely effect on others and then she freely decides to bear the child for that other woman. The gametes from which the child is formed may came from the other woman and her husband and by the use of *in vitro* fertilisation an embryo may be formed and then transferred into her. She is then bearing the 'genetic child' of the other woman for her. Or she may contribute her own oocyte while the husband of the other woman contributes the sperm and the embryo may be formed by ivf and then transferred into her. What is morally wrong, intrinsically immoral, with what the woman is doing? What moral principle is she flouting? In the example I have cited the surrogate mother sees herself as engaging in a purely altruistic act, bringing a child into existence for her sister or friend or some other needy person. In a very real sense she is animated by a 'pro-life' attitude since she is creating a child and so allowing a family to be formed. If it is noble to put one's life at risk for a friend, why is it not noble to use one's womb for a friend? Is the surrogate mother wrong about this, or misguided?

In the past, of course, surrogacy involved actual sexual intercourse with the husband of the infertile woman and one might perhaps see this as a form of fornication or adultery, although of course neither party had the intention of violating the marriage bond nor of engaging in sexual intercourse outside marriage in the usual sense. One could hardly call the surrogate mother or the husband of the infertile woman 'unfaithful'. (It is worth remarking that in the Old Testament surrogacy is not seen as a form either of fornication or of adultery.) Now, however, surrogacy usually involves artificial insemination, or the use of IVF where the ovum and sperm of the infertile couple can be used to create an embryo *in vitro* which is then transferred to the surrogate mother.

Whatever one may think about artificial insemination, it can hardly be seen as either an act of fornication or an act of adultery involving of itself a disruption to or alienation of the relationship between husband and wife on both sides of the arrangement. And in the case of IVF assisted surrogacy, where the embryo may be formed from the ovum and sperm of the infertile couple themselves and then implanted in the surrogate mother, it can hardly be argued that this of itself involves some kind of violent interference in the relationship between husband and wife. (In the Vatican *Instruction on Respect for Human Life* (1987) Cardinal Ratzinger speaks as though the medical practitioners of assisted reproduction physically come between the partners in their reproductive acts and in some way violate the 'unitive' body-to-body intimacy of the sexual embrace.) Rather, they are using the IVF technology to help them achieve their own purposes as a married couple. In fact the whole purpose and intention of the surrogacy arrangement is to help and foster the relationship between the infertile husband and wife by allowing them to overcome their infertility and so to form a family. In a very real sense the intention of the couple and of the surrogate mother is 'pro life'. Discussing artificial insemination, the French moral theologian Patrick Verspieren SJ argues that donor insemination does not involve 'adultery':

> It is true that in both cases if the woman becomes pregnant it is due to germ cells from a man who is not her partner. But in adultery there is a sexual encounter between the woman and the other man and a conjunction of their bodies expressing and symbolising their mutual (albeit transitory) desire; or, at the least, a relation between the two is created, no matter how ephemeral it might be. Recourse to artificial insemination, on the other hand, is the expression of an intention of conjugal fidelity. The couple could have separated and they have not done so; the woman could have sought to become pregnant in the course of an 'adventure' and the man could have accepted her infidelity more or less willingly, but both refused this.

The same author notes that in France the incidence of divorce among couples who employ artificial insemination is much less than that in the general population.[10]

These objections to surrogacy — that it involves fornication or adultery — do not then have very much force, especially for those who do not have a specifically Christian view of sexuality and marriage. The principal objection is, of course, the one mentioned before, namely that surrogacy involves one person (the infertile mother) using another person (the surrogate mother) as a means to her ends. In effect, it is claimed the surrogate mother is treated as a thing, an instrument, and not as a person. The Warnock Committee in its celebrated report used this argument against surrogacy, and others have argued that surrogacy is 'akin to slavery', meaning presumably that the surrogate mother is being used as a 'slave' for the infertile mother.

Kant was of course one of the first to formulate the principle behind this argument: one must never treat another person merely as a means to one's own ends but rather as an end in himself or herself. But, it is not easy to formulate the principle appropriately since there are clearly occasions where it is quite moral to employ another person to perform some service for reward. For example, I can employ someone to carry bricks for me or dig trenches for me — a 'surrogate' brick carrier or trench digger — so long as he freely consents and so long as I pay him appropriately. Again, I can accept services offered altruistically to me (for example, a friend might offer to look after my children for me) without necessarily using or exploiting that person as a means to my ends or using him or her as a thing or instrument. Exploitation arises only if the one whom I employ or who offers services to me is coerced in some way, either by direct force or situationally through, for example, poverty, unequal power, psychological or social or familial blackmail, so that he or she does not really consent freely to work for me or render services to me.

Slavery is precisely the situation where a person is made to serve another by force or coercion and where no kind of free and informed consent has been possible. Some ordinary marriages are exploitative in this way, in that the woman is forced into the marriage either directly or situationally, or through family pressures, and is used by the husband as a means to his ends, as a piece of property, as a domestic slave, as a sexual object. In the same way, some surrogacy arrangements may also be exploitative in that the surrogate mother is coerced, either directly or indirectly, to bear a child for another. But it is difficult to see that *all* marriages and *all* surrogacy arrangements must necessarily be like this. In order to use Kant's principle against surrogacy one would have to show that surrogacy necessarily and of itself involves the coercion of one woman by another, directly or indirectly, so that the surrogate could not really make a free decision to bear a child for another. It is obvious, however, that many women do make such free decisions to act as surrogate mothers and that one cannot simply assume that they are all unwilling and unfree 'slaves' serving the purposes of other people. (It has been estimated that in the US as of 1987 some seventeen surrogacy programs had arranged up to 4000 births. The total number of births through surrogacy arrangements would of course be larger than this if one took into account informal arrangements which are not notified publicly.)

Surrogacy then does not of itself necessarily involve one woman being used as a means to serve the ends of other people and this argument against the practice of surrogate motherhood fails. It might be replied, however, that while surrogacy may not of itself involve the surrogate being used or exploited, nevertheless in the concrete social circumstances in which we find ourselves, surrogacy is likely to be used in an exploitative way.

This is in fact the position of the feminist movement known as FINRRAGE (the Feminist International Network of Resistance to Reproductive and Genetic Engineering). According to this view,

> infertility is a problem for women only because they live in a society which encourages women to see themselves as nothing more than potential mothers. It is the failure of women to view themselves as anything more than potential mothers that leads to their wish to use reproductive technologies to fulfil a particular limited vision of themselves. Rather than encouraging women to do so, we should work to transform society in such a way that women do not feel they have to be mothers ... Some argue that the medical profession succeeds in entrapping women into their programmes because effectively brainwashed infertile women will do anything to have children.[11]

In this view then women are incapable of making truly free and informed decisions, and the new forms of assisted procreation or reproductive technologies, including surrogacy, and the new ways of birth and family formation they make possible are not really means of liberation for women but rather are new forms of oppression by which women are locked into the role of potential mother. Surrogate mothers may think that they are being altruistic in helping other women to have children but what they are doing in reality is helping to reinforce the oppressive stereotype of woman as mother.

By any measure this is an extraordinary argument. It may be that in some cases the desire to overcome one's infertility is simply an unthinking response to social and cultural pressures. But in many cases the wish to have a child is simply a very human desire, and it is difficult to imagine why anyone should think that they have a right to tell an infertile woman that she has been brainwashed into thinking that she wants to have a child, or to tell a woman who offers to bear a child for another that she does not know what she is doing, or to accuse her of letting down the women's cause, or to move so that she should be legally prevented from choosing to act as a surrogate mother. One might think that feminists who invoke the 'pro choice' principle with regard to abortion and sexual lifestyle (including the right of lesbian couples to have children by artificial insemination) would see the same principle as applying to the decision of a woman to bear a child for another. If a woman is capable of making an autonomous decision to have an abortion, or to form a lesbian union and have children within such a union, it is difficult to see why a woman cannot make an autonomous decision to bear a child for another woman. If one adopts a pro choice principle, that a woman has the right to use her body as she chooses, then one must be consistent. One cannot use the principle to justify a woman's right to have an abortion and so to prevent a child from coming into existence and then reject it vis-à-vis a woman's right to enter into a surrogacy arrangement and so to bring a child into existence.

It is difficult, then, to see that there are any convincing arguments of moral principle against surrogate motherhood. It does not of itself necessarily involve treating women as means to the ends of other women, or exploiting them, or treating them as

80

'slaves'. On the contrary it affirms the 'pro choice' principle that a woman should be allowed to choose for herself how she is going to use her body, and it affirms the 'pro life' principle that having children is a central human good.

Consequences of surrogacy

We turn now to the arguments against surrogacy based upon the alleged consequences of the practice for both the surrogate mother and the child born of a surrogacy arrangement. As was remarked before, in this kind of consequentialist argument it is not enough to show that surrogacy may *possibly* lead to some deleterious consequences for both surrogate mothers and the children they bear for others; one must show that there is actual evidence to suggest that it does lead to such consequences typically or in most cases, and that these consequences are so serious and of such magnitude as to warrant intervention by the state to prohibit the practice. One must also show that, if it is allowed, surrogacy is likely to become a widespread form of family formation. When one looks at the arguments, however, little hard evidence is brought forward to show that surrogacy does in fact have the serious and malign consequences it is supposed to have. A recent report of a committee of the Anglican Archdiocese of Melbourne in Australia says, for example, that surrogacy involves such deleterious consequences for the child in terms of its sense of its own identity (who is my real mother and whose child am I?) and for the surrogate mother regarding her 'possible manipulation ... within the context of emotional family relationships', that it should be severely discouraged by the community. (It should be mentioned that the committee thinks that it would be practically futile for the state to prohibit altruistic or non-commercial surrogacy, or to subject participants in surrogacy arrangements to criminal penalties.) The committee also expresses the fear that if altruistic surrogacy is allowed this will be a thin end of the wedge for the introduction of commercial surrogacy which is, in their words, 'akin to slavery'.[12]

One might expect that such large and confident claims about surrogacy would be supported by empirical evidence about its psychological effects on children or about the manipulation of women in family contexts. One might also expect some comparisons to be made with what happens in 'ordinary' marriage and family relationships, to see whether children born from surrogacy arrangements are any worse off psychologically than children born from ordinary families, or from single parent situations, or from artificial insemination, or from lesbian unions, or from reconstituted families after divorce and remarriage. But no such evidence is ever offered. There is, it seems, some evidence to suggest that children who are adopted are statistically more likely to have psychological problems than children born within 'ordinary' family situations, but no one has so far advocated that this is so typical and so large a problem that the practice of adoption should be banned. (What it does imply is that we should be more careful about the adoption process with regard to the problems of adopted children and relinquishing mothers.) There is, of course, a great deal of evidence to show the deleterious effects of divorce and family break-up on children, but once again no one has advocated that this is an argument for prohibiting divorce and marriage break-up. To repeat the point made before, what the consequentialist has to show is that the practice of surrogacy actually has such undesirable consequences, both for the child and the surrogate mother of the child, of such seriousness and magnitude that the law should, as with open access to hard drugs, prohibit it. It might be mentioned in this connection that out of 4000 recorded surrogate births in recent years in the US only one per cent have resulted in litigation.[13]

It is apposite here to say something about the principle that the best interests of the child should be considered to be paramount when one is considering surrogacy. This principle is primarily a legal maxim which applies to cases concerning the custody of children after divorce and marriage break-up; it also applies to adoption processes and to cases where the child is removed from its parents' care in cases of neglect or abuse.[14] In those contexts the maxim has a completely clear meaning, namely that the child who is already in existence has interests and rights of its own which must be taken into account. But it has been given the status of an absolute principle by some and used to argue that surrogacy is necessarily and always against the best interests of the child and so should be prohibited. Better that the child not exist at all rather than be born of a surrogacy arrangement.

At times it seems to be suggested the child born of a surrogacy arrangement is necessarily being used as a means to the infertile mother's end and so is not, according to Kant's principle, being treated as a person in its own right. The infertile woman is painted as selfishly pursuing what she thinks is her 'right' to have a child. However, the child of a surrogacy arrangement is in most cases brought into existence simply because an infertile woman wants to have a child in exactly the same way that fertile women want to have children. She does not claim a 'right' to have a child, any more than a fertile woman claims such a right. What exactly is the difference in intention between a woman having a child through a surrogacy arrangement and having a child in the ordinary way? A couple may, in the ordinary situation, wish to have a child for a variety of reasons, some altruistic and some self interested. No doubt in some cases a child may be brought into existence to provide another pair of hands to work, to provide psychological support for a fragile marriage, to take the place of a dead sibling and so on. But in the ideal situation a couple will want to bring a child into existence as a manifestation of their love for one another and out of a disinterested wish to give life to a new human being. Similarly, there is no reason why an infertile couple cannot in the same loving and altruistic spirit wish to have a child and accept the offer of a surrogate mother to bear a child for them. The child of a surrogacy arrangement is no more a means to an end than is the child of an ordinary marriage. One can imagine a mother saying to her child born from a surrogacy arrangement: 'I wasn't able to bear you myself but another woman offered to bear you for me and I wanted you so much that I accepted her offer. What I did and what she did was done out of love for you'.

As an American philosopher, Laura M. Purdy, has put it:

> Considering the sorts of reasons why parents have children, it is hard to see why the idea that one was conceived in order to provide a desperately wanted child to another is thought to be problematic. One might well prefer that to the idea that one was an 'accident', adopted, born because contraception or abortion were not available, conceived to cement a failing marriage, to continue a family line, to qualify for welfare aid, to sex balance a family, or as an experiment in child rearing. Surely what matters for a child's well-being in the end is whether it is being raised in a loving, intelligent environment.[15]

It is, then, simply not true that a child born of a surrogacy arrangement is necessarily being treated as a means to some other's end and as an instrument or exchangeable commodity or non-person. The child born of a surrogacy arrangement is no more the 'property' of the commissioning parents than is the child of ordinary parents: it has exactly the same rights as the latter.

Another version of the best interests of the child argument is that being born from a surrogacy arrangement is likely to have such damaging psychological effects on the child that surrogacy should not be allowed. In other words, it is argued that the effects on a child will be so devastating that it is better that the child not be born at all. This argument has already been discussed and it has been noted that there is absolutely no evidence to show that the sense of personal identity of children born from surrogacy arrangements is so severely damaged that such children should not be brought into existence. (It might be noted in parenthesis that this argument is often used by 'pro life' people who nevertheless argue that women may, even should, bring into existence children suffering from grave physical and mental handicaps, for example where the mother is a carrier of some severe genetic disease.) Again, as noted before, children who are adopted, or who have been born through artificial insemination or through IVF by donated gametes, may suffer from psychological problems about their personal identity, but we don't use this to argue that these modes of family formation should be banned. What then, we may ask, is so different about surrogacy that it should be legally prohibited?

Finally, while we are considering the supposed consequences of surrogacy, something must be said about the alleged social effects of the legal toleration of surrogacy. One gets the impression from some statements concerning surrogacy that allowing the practice will subvert the central values of our society and the basic institutions of marriage and the family. But once again there is no evidence to support this claim. Surrogate parenting programs have been in existence in the US for over ten years and in the states where surrogacy is legally allowed there do not appear to have been the dire social effects spoken about. Again, the number of couples involved in surrogacy arrangements is still relatively small even in those states where there is legal toleration of surrogacy. In Australia there are no statistics but, on the evidence the former National Bioethics Consultative Committee was able to collect, it would seem that ten to fifteen couples might use this method of forming a family in a year. Given the difficulties of making a surrogacy arrangement, surrogacy is never going to be a preferred means of having a child and forming a family. It will always be a last resort for very few couples. It is, then, hard to imagine that allowing ten or so people per annum to form families through surrogacy arrangements is likely to open the floodgates and bring about the subversion of marriage and the family.

As mentioned before, there are already many alternative means of family formation accepted in our society — adoption, donor insemination, IVF using donor gametes, single parents, homosexual parents, family reconstitution after divorce — and it is very difficult to see why surrogacy as a means of family formation should be singled out and so unequivocally rejected. It has been claimed that surrogacy represents 'an experiment with family relationships', and in a sense it is; but there are many other experiments with family relationships which have been accepted by our society and there is no evidence to show that surrogacy is a notably more dangerous 'experiment' than the others.

The third and final issue concerns personal morality and the law. Even if one could show that surrogate motherhood were ethically undesirable it would not follow automatically — at least in a liberal society — that it should be prohibited by the law. For that it would be necessary to show that it involved obvious and direct harm of a serious and large-scale kind to other people, that it would be practicable to enforce the prohibition and that enforcing it would not bring about more evil than good. (A number of church committees have recognised it would not be practicable to try to prohibit surrogacy directly and they propose ways of severely discouraging the practice by, for example, making any medical practitioner assisting a surrogacy arrangement guilty of gross misconduct, or by requiring the commissioning parents to go through adoption procedures in order to became the legal parents of the child.) But in a liberal society where a special value is given to personal freedom and where it is recognised that people may freely choose to procreate and form families in a number of different ways, it also needs to be shown that choosing to form a family by using surrogacy arrangements involves anti-social consequences of a large and obvious kind, before one seeks to prohibit it by law.

It is difficult not to see the choice of the infertile couple to enter into a surrogacy arrangement, and the choice of a surrogate mother to offer to bear a child for them, as being wholly within the sphere of personal morality which it is not the law's business to enter. The state has of course the right to regulate the practice, as it does with adoption, artificial insemination, IVF and

other modes of family formation, but it does not have the right
to prohibit it. The state might, for example, make provision for
counselling women entering surrogacy arrangements to ensure
that they are capable of making free and informed decisions; for
keeping records of the birth circumstances of children born
from such arrangements; and for ensuring that there is an adequate interval between the birth of a child and its being handed
over to the social parents in order to allow the surrogate mother
to make a considered final decision.

In our pluralist society people have very different views about
a range of moral issues to do with sexuality, reproduction and
family formation, and we have in many cases to agree to disagree. Some Christians, in particular Roman Catholic Christians,
find it hard to accept this fact and they think that those who are
willing to allow abortion, or who support the rights of homosexuals, or who endorse the use of the new reproductive technologies, or recognise the new modes of family formation,
including surrogate motherhood, are motivated by some kind of
ill will or subscribe to some form of moral libertarianism that
means anything goes in the ethical sphere. But respect for
and toleration of the conscientious moral and religious views
of other people, even when they are completely counter to
Christian views, have always been part of the mainstream
Catholic tradition, and that applies to the different modes of
family formation, including surrogate motherhood, as much as
anything else. From this point of view there is no difficulty in
Christians generally, and Roman Catholics in particular, acknowledging (while quite properly having their own grave moral
reservations about) the conscientious right of infertile people to
have children through surrogacy arrangements or the right of a
woman to offer to bear a child for them. Some Christians may
choose not to use surrogacy arrangements for themselves, nor to
act as surrogate mothers, but they should respect the conscientious decision of others to do so.

At present, many people's attitudes to the right of a woman to bear a child for another if she so chooses are quite illiberal in that they effectively deny the moral autonomy of the woman. They need to be reminded that they are living in a liberal society.

Feminist views on reproductive technology

Certain feminist views have already been mentioned in the discussion on surrogacy. One might have expected that the right which has played a central part in the feminist movement, that women have final control over their own bodies and their reproductive processes, would have been invoked apropos of surrogacy. This right is a direct corollary of the fact that women are autonomous moral agents and is simply a version of the general principle of autonomy. If a woman is not able to use her body as she wishes, so long as no harm is done to others, and if she is not able to control her reproductive capacities as she freely chooses, she is no longer in responsible control of a vitally significant part of her life. (In a sense this is not an exclusively women's right since it applies equally to men; but it applies of course in a special way to women.)

In parenthesis, it might be remarked that the principle that a woman may use her body as she chooses has been used mainly with respect to abortion, but it is complicated in that situation since the right of the mother to control her body and her reproductive processes, and to have an abortion, is in conflict with the quasi-right of the fetus (which will, all things being equal, become or develop into a human being) to continued life. There is no way *in principle* in which this conflict can be resolved so that in all cases the mother's right to control her bodily and reproductive processes takes precedence over the right of the fetus, or vice versa. All that can be done is to weigh the two principles with respect to the particular circumstances. Thus, for example, if a woman's pregnancy were the result of rape or incest it would seem that her right to control her body as she chooses (and to have an abortion) should take precedence (at the cost of denying the quasi-right of the fetus to continued life); but if the pregnancy were in the last trimester it would seem that the right of the fetus should take precedence (at the cost of coercing the mother, against her will, to continue the pregnancy).

However, as we have seen, some women have taken a different view of surrogacy and of reproductive technology or assisted procreation in general and there is now a wide range of feminist views about these matters. It is worthwhile looking at these views in a detailed way since they exhibit some of the complexities of applying the concept of autonomy in this area.

The feminist voice — or better, feminist voices — have played a significant part in the debate over the moral and social implications of the new reproductive technologies. Since women are affected by *in vitro* fertilisation and other forms of reproductive technology in a much more direct and momentous way than men, it is altogether to be expected that they will be major contributors to the discussion. To some degree, it is true, the male experience in reproductive technology has been neglected: infertile men often choose to undergo difficult and recurrent surgery to remedy their infertility and, so it has been said, 'male emotions, desires and anger (apropos infertility) are equal to that of the female, albeit expressed differently'.[16] Nevertheless, it remains true that it is women who usually have to undergo the major medical procedures and who bear the children brought into being by the new birth technologies. It is their bodies which are, so to speak, in contention.

When women speak about these technologies then their views deserve special attention. The fact is, however, that they speak in a variety of different voices. Carol Gilligan's celebrated book, *In a Different Voice*, argues that women have a distinctive form of experience of their own and a distinctive expression of that experience.[17] However, over the last twenty years feminist responses to the new birth technologies have undergone a radical series of changes and there is now a genuine 'pluralism' of voices and views. They are, no doubt, still distinctively feminist views and they bear a 'family resemblance' to each other, but they are also very different from each other. (It is for that reason that, in what follows, I cite at some length from the various feminist writings.)

Some feminist thinkers have traced these developments to demographic and social changes among middle-class women over the last twenty years. Thus, three English feminists observe that:

> in the early 1970s, when the current wave of feminism began, most of the women involved in the movement had had their children and were searching for other means of fulfilment in their lives, or had not had children and were not yet having to face the issue of whether they ever would choose to be mothers. Both groups saw it important to prove that women did not have to be seen only in terms of their reproductive abilities. For both groups, reproductive freedom meant freedom *from* reproduction.[18]

However, these authors go on, some women of this group are now more interested in having children because they are growing older — women in their twenties in the 1970s can no longer delay child bearing and have to make a decision — and because of changes in the political climate. 'Feminism', they say, 'is no longer for many women the totally absorbing activity and form of self-definition it once was. Feminists, like others, may be turning inwards to rear children, perhaps as the only social contribution to make in a period of reaction and political quiescence.' As a result, they conclude,

> Babies themselves, not just the limitations they impose on their mothers' lives, have after a period of near oblivion, become a matter of interest to the women's movement. And this has led a few feminists to experience problems with their own infertility, and even more to take an interest in the issues surrounding pregnancy and childbirth, including infertility and its treatment.[19]

Quite apart from these factors, there has been a natural movement of critical revisionism within feminism. All revolutionary movements, whether they are political, religious or philosophical, usually begin with absolute and unilateral positions; they then pass through a reflective and critical revisionist phase to a more pluralist position characterised by the emergence and acceptance of differing perspectives and interpretive frameworks. This kind of development is clearly observable in many religious movements, as well as in philosophical movements like Marxism and Freudianism, and it is not surprising that it is now appearing within feminism. One could, in fact, apply to the feminist movement as a whole the observation by Carol Gilligan that personal cognitive maturity involves 'changes in thinking that mark the transition from a belief that knowledge is absolute and answers clearly right or wrong to an understanding of the contextual relativity of both truth and choice'.[20]

Some may see this as a sign of incoherence and confusion within the feminist position, but that would be a mistake. In fact it is an index of maturity in any movement — religious, political, artistic, feminist — that it is ready to eschew a strictly monolithic position and tolerate, even welcome, a variety of views and positions. Pluralism is a sign of vitality and strength, not of exhaustion, weakness and confusion.

In the early 1970s a number of feminist thinkers welcomed the advent of the new reproductive technologies as a means of liberation for women from the tyranny of their biological nature which condemned them to pregnancy and child bearing and rearing. For example, the American writer Shulamith Firestone argued in her book *The Dialectic of Sex*[21] that artificial reproduction would eventually allow women to escape the 'barbaric' state of pregnancy. This in turn would allow women to overcome their oppressed social position which is a direct consequence of their biology. Firestone's position, and that of other 'first wave' feminists who shared her views, rested upon a naively optimistic view of technology, as though it were value-neutral and could be used at will by women for their own liberationist ends. In the 1970s and 1980s, however, the critique of this view of technology by thinkers such as Langdon Winner, Jacques Ellul and others showed how deeply the various forms of technology are already pervaded by socio-political values and how difficult it is to make technology serve the cause of human liberation. The techno-pessimism, as one may call it, that emerged from this critique combined with the environmentalist movement to show that in many cases the technology that was supposed to free us from the determinisms of nature in fact enslaved us further.

This critical and pessimistic attitude to technology was taken over in the 1980s by a number of feminist thinkers vis-à-vis the new reproductive technologies. The older, naively optimistic view that these technologies were an instrument of liberation for women (like the new contraceptive and abortifacient technologies) was rejected and they were now seen as a means for males to oppress women under the guise of liberating them. The new technologies involved women's bodies being used by male scientists for research and, at a deeper level, they were an attempt to deprive women of power over their most distinctive capacity, reproduction, and make it subject to male control.

A further element in this argument is that infertile women are led to submit themselves to this kind of scientific exploitation because the 'pro-natalist' pressures of our society make them see reproduction as bound up with their identity as women. As we have seen apropos of certain feminist criticisms of surrogate motherhood, a quasi-Marxist idea of 'false consciousness' was also introduced in order to explain many women's desire to have children. They may really think that they have such a desire but they are not aware that it is a 'false desire' induced in them by society: it is, to use a modish (and misleading) term, 'socially constructed'. Further, by satisfying their own self-interested personal wishes to have a child through IVF they are conniving in the larger exploitation of women and betraying a lack of feminine class consciousness. As Mara Mies has said, 'any woman who is prepared to have a child manufactured for her by a fame-and money-greedy biotechnician must know that in this way she is not only fulfilling her own individual, often egoistic wish to have a baby, but also surrendering yet another part of the autonomy of the female sex over child-bearing to the techno-patriarchs'.[22]

This false consciousness on the part of women who resort to IVF and other forms of reproductive technology in turn provides a basis for legitimate paternalism since women in this situation do not really know what is for their own good or for the common good of women as a whole and they have to be prevented, for their own good and the good of women as a class, from using the new reproductive technologies. Another feature of this general position is its tendency to invent what might be called Orwellian scenarios, where the future horrors of reproductive technology — mechanical wombs, using 'neo-morts' as fetal incubators, gendercide through sex selection — are imaginatively conjured up. The most dramatic of these scenarios is the 'reproductive brothel' of Gena Corea: 'While sexual prostitutes sell vagina, rectum and mouth, reproductive prostitutes will sell other body parts: womb, ovaries, eggs'.[23] This general position was espoused by other feminist thinkers in the early 1980s, such as Mary O'Brien and Christine Overall,[24] and one of its main expressions is to be found in the FINRRAGE movement. One of the curious features of this movement is that it has found itself in coalition not just, as one would expect, with the Green movement but also with conservative Catholics and fundamentalist Christians who are in most other respects (for example on abortion and female homosexuality) totally at odds with the radical feminist position. Thus, for example, the Vatican rejection of IVF was welcomed by some members of FINRRAGE and they have also found common cause with conservative Christian views on embryo experimentation and surrogate motherhood.

This of course does not constitute an objection to their position; however what is more difficult to explain is why the technology of IVF and the other forms of assisted procreation were singled out for opposition. After all, the contraceptive pill and other means of contraception are also forms of technology, as are the various forms of abortifacients. These kinds of technology are also part of 'male patriarchalist science' and involve the intervention of men in the process of reproduction and the use of women in scientific experimentation, but they are not seen by these feminists as attempts to deprive women of their reproductive powers. Contraceptive and abortifacient technologies which enable women *not* to have children are seen as conducive to women's liberation (although there have been feminist criticisms of male insensitivities in contraceptive research and development). Again, women who use contraceptive and abortifacient technologies are not presumed to be victims of false consciousness, nor accused of letting the collective feminist cause down, nor seen to be in need of paternalistic advice and direction (even legal coercion). They are, it seems to have been assumed, capable of autonomous decision-making about contraceptive and abortifacient technology in a way in which they are not capable of freely and autonomously choosing for themselves about reproductive technology.

It is interesting to look in detail at the arguments used by proponents of this position against surrogacy and embryo experimentation. As we have seen, with regard to the question of surrogate motherhood some feminists of this persuasion have argued that it is impossible for a woman to choose freely and autonomously to act as a surrogate mother and to bear a child for another woman. There are two variants of this argument: first, that surrogate motherhood is *of itself* so exploitative of women that it cannot be freely chosen, any more than a person could freely choose to be a slave; second, that *in the present social situation* it is not possible for a woman freely and autonomously to choose to bear a child for another. The first variant is represented by Christine Overall, who claims that 'there is a real moral danger in the type of conceptual framework that presents surrogate motherhood as even a possible freely chosen alternative for women'.[25] The second is represented by Susan Dodds and Karen Jones, who argue that in our present social situation 'it is unlikely that many women can make an autonomous choice to enter into a surrogacy contract which would compel them to surrender the child at birth'.[26] These authors do not argue that

94

surrogacy as such should not be chosen as an option by a woman, but that in the present situation of society, where women are oppressed and exploited, they should not make such decisions. This in turn legitimates paternalistic action by the state to prevent women choosing to bear children for other women.

> If the world were different, a policy of making surrogacy contracts illegal might not be necessary. If surrogacy agreements were clearly not exploitative offers, and if monitoring occurred to ensure that a decision to become a surrogate reflected and protected a woman's autonomy, then, perhaps, such agreements would be viable. However, that is not the present situation, and so surrogacy contracts must become not only unenforceable, but, as they pay insufficient regard for the resultant child and tend to risk commodifying both women and children, illegal.[27]

This strongly paternalistic attitude goes together, in some feminist arguments, with a critique of an 'individualistic' concept of rights and of moral 'libertarianism' based upon the principle of autonomy. To the objection that feminist views on contraception and abortion rely upon the right of a woman to choose whether or not to have a child and upon the autonomy of women in respect of their control over their own bodies, one answer is that abortion is often a socially responsible act and is not justified solely in terms of the individualistic right of a woman to do what she wants to do with her own body. As it has been put: abortion is 'an act of social responsibility with respect to family formation'.[28] It is not clear, however, why the use of abortifacient technology in order *not* to have a child is an 'act of social responsibility' and why the use of reproductive technology in order to *have* a child is an act of irresponsible individualism.

With regard to IVF and embryo experimentation, some feminists subscribing to the position just outlined oppose such experimentation not because the IVF embryo is seen as a human person with the same right to life as a fully formed human person, but rather because embryos come from the ova 'harvested' from women's bodies, so the latter become experimental 'sites' for reproductive scientists. The use of superovulatory drugs and invasive surgical techniques also means that women become experimental 'fodder'. As it has been put by Robyn Rowland,

> The feminist position on embryo experimentation does not recognise the embryo as a separate human entity. It makes both women and the social context central to its position. Few protagonists in the embryo experimentation debate ask where the embryos came from. They come from eggs. And where do the eggs come from? They come from women's bodies.[29]

These feminists are also concerned that this kind of experimentation will lead to gender selection of early embryos, with the consequence that female embryos will be systematically eliminated in favour of male embryos. In other words, we will end with a form of 'gendercide'.

In general, this feminist position claims that 'IVF is an unsuccessful technology that threatens the freedom and the well-being of women, and that only a few white, middle-class heterosexual couples will benefit from IVF, along with the shareholders of genetic engineering companies. A woman's participation in reproductive technology is thus the result of conforming to the whims of male domination'.[30]

'Third wave' feminist views

This stringent critique of reproductive technology was, perhaps, the dominant view in 'second wave' feminist thinking through the 1980s and still retains a good deal of influence. However, there are now signs that the absolute rejection of reproductive technology is being critically reassessed by some recent feminists. These thinkers reject the naive optimism of early feminists such as Firestone and recognise with Corea that the new technology is not value-neutral but is in fact pervaded by certain technocratic values, and that there are real dangers of its being used against women in an exploitative way. At the same time they argue that the reproductive technologies can be used to help women achieve liberation if they are able to control those technologies for their own purposes. If the 'pro choice' principle governs women's access to the new forms of contraception and to improved ways of abortion — both brought about by medical technology — why should it not govern women's access to IVF and other forms of birth technology, provided that there is a real choice for the women concerned?

A good example of this development in feminist thinking is the recently published *Tomorrow's Child: Reproductive Technology in the 1990s* by the three well known English feminists mentioned before. In the preface to their book, Birke, Himmelweit and Vines characterise the FINRRAGE position as being dominated by fear — 'fear that what we are witnessing is a takeover by scientists of women's role in reproduction, and fear that we are moving towards a dehumanised (and defeminised) technological future. The position is one of total resistance to scientific and male control of reproductive processes, by a complete rejection of the new technologies'. As against this, the authors affirm the primacy of the feminist principle 'that women should be able to choose whether or not to bear a child': 'We feel that women, and women alone, should be the ones to make the choice'.[31] At the same time these authors adopt an attitude of healthy scepticism towards some of the more extreme reproductive scenarios (the possibility of ectogenesis and the mechanical womb, the use of ova donation and embryo transfer to create Corea's and Dworkin's 'reproductive brothel'). They also question the version of Murphy's Law which a good deal of previous feminist thinking has invoked: if a biotechnological development is theoretically possible it is likely actually to occur and it is bound to be bad for women. This is, the authors argue, to adopt an unduly pessimistic view in that it assumes that women are unable to resist pressures from male medical technocrats and are incapable of exercising autonomy and taking control of the technology themselves (as has happened to some extent in ordinary birthing practices).

In the conclusion to their book the authors set out a number of 'feminist principles' which supplement the 'pro choice' principle and provide a social and political dimension to their discussion. Reproductive politics, they say, must find ways of changing the arrangements for reproduction in our society which are oppressive to women, and of enabling women to carry out effectively their reproductive choices. A similar view has been taken by the American feminist philosopher Mary Anne Warren, who argues that while 'the costs and risks of IVF treatments to the female patient are substantial . . . they are not known to be so great as to clearly outweigh the potential benefits, in every case'.[32] 'There are physical and social dangers for women in reproductive technology but women can by various means attempt to contain these dangers rather than seeking to eliminate the new technologies altogether. They must also work to gain more control of the technologies'. Warren says that 'it is too soon to conclude that this new reproductive technology will not serve women's interests . . . If women and other underprivileged groups can gain a larger presence in the medical and research professions, and if suitable modes of regulation can be implemented, then the new reproductive technologies may provide more benefits than dangers.'[33] Again, another feminist philosopher, Laura Purdy, argues against the position that surrogacy is necessarily opposed to women's best interests. As she puts it:

> That surrogacy reduces rather than promotes women's autonomy may be true under some circumstances, but there are good grounds for thinking that it can also enhance autonomy. It also remains to be shown that the practice systematically burdens women, or one class of women. In principle, the availability of new choices can be expected to nourish rather than stunt women's lives, so long as they retain control over their bodies and their lives. The claim that contracted pregnancy destroys women's individuality and constitutes alienated labour, as Christine Overall argues, depends not only on

a problematic Marxist analysis, but on the assumption that other jobs available to women are seriously less alienating.[34]

An optimistic view of the 'procreative technologies' and of surrogate motherhood is also put forward by the American legal scholar Lisa C. Ikemoto, who argues that they 'increase availability of choice, thereby increasing the opportunity for women to achieve autonomy through decision-making. This in turn advances sexual equality'. Ikemoto goes on:

> Some feminists have disparaged the institution of motherhood by stating that it prevents women from achieving equality. Other women, including feminists, see it in more positive terms. Surrogate motherhood gives infertile women or women who fear transmitting deleterious genes a chance to enjoy the child-rearing aspect of motherhood. No less important is that surrogate motherhood constitutes a vehicle for a woman to help another woman in a uniquely feminine way, by carrying her child.[35]

A different kind of argument about surrogacy has been proposed by the Australian sociologist and feminist Sharyn L. Roach Anleu. This author argues that the distinction between commercial and altruistic surrogacy is neither self-evident nor natural but in fact reflects and reinforces gender norms. Altruistic surrogacy is seen as belonging to the private domestic sphere where relationships 'are supposed to be based on affection and emotion which are private, irrational sentiments, thereby inappropriate subjects for legal regulation'.[36] It is therefore more accepted, or at least not so sharply condemned, as commercial surrogacy. 'In a sense', Roach Anleu concludes,

> surrogacy is an extension of the kinds of nurturing related activities women have always performed, such as child rearing, which have not always been recognised as compensatable work, but treated as resulting from natural female emotions and instincts. Paid surrogacy breaks the myth of the maternal instinct; not only can women have babies and give them away, but they can also enter into a contract that actually rewards them for having babies. Anything less

99

than that is exploitation because the notion of altruistic choice is socially constructed and reinforces gender norms; payment for services questions gender norms.[37]

Birke, Himmelweit and Vines make the same point about the private–public distinction. Commercial or contractual surrogacy, they say, offends people because it represents 'an overstepping of the boundaries between public and private, the introduction of the public way of getting people to do things by paying them money, into an activity which is supposed to remain within the private sphere.[38] Feminists, they conclude, 'should be suspicious of such distinctions; the division between public and private has on the whole been oppressive to women and has been used to keep them out of the public arena'.[39]

With regard to the issue of embryo experimentation, Karen Dawson and Beth Gaze accept the claim of Robyn Rowland and others that the present debate is focussed too much on the embryo, without taking into account the woman who supplies the ovum and who is the subject of research. However, they argue, 'the separation of embryo research from the woman's treatment has led to a situation where women undergoing IVF treatment continue to accept the transfer of potentially defective embryos and the possibility of miscarriage, therapeutic abortion, or giving birth to a child with congenital abnormalities, because of their commitment to the goal of having a child'. If this situation is to be remedied and women protected, some embryo research and experimentation must be carried out.[40]

In an essay entitled 'Is IVF a threat to women's autonomy?' Mary Anne Warren claims that women are able to make free and autonomous decisions about donating embryos for research and experimentation. At the same time she lays down a number of prescriptions to be observed by reproductive scientists and technologists in order to ensure that the women in IVF programs give genuinely informed consent to the procedure.[41] What is essential is that IVF, embryo experimentation and all the other procedures connected with IVF should as far as possible be in the control of women. Warren uses very much the same kind of argument in a study of gender selection and the danger of 'gendercide':

> Sex selection is not always sexist, socially harmful, or disrespectful of the child as an end in itself. Its sexism and its potential for harm are very much a function of how it is done, why it is done, and the social context. That being the case, universal condemnation seems inappropriate, and regulation preferable, at least in the first instance, to prohibition.[42]

The 'third wave' feminists just mentioned do not constitute a 'school' or a 'movement'. Nevertheless, there are certain common features in their approaches to the new reproductive technologies. First, they are critical of any absolute and unilateral rejection of the new technologies and of the techno-pessimism which sees them as beyond any kind of control by women. Control, they suggest, is what is needed, not condemnation or prohibition. At the same time, they recognise the difficulties in the way of achieving informed decision-making and control by women. This group is also sceptical of the Orwellian future scenarios imagined by Corea and others of the FINRRAGE group, and they are critical of the paternalistic attitudes of the same group which, as has been said, are 'insulting' to infertile women. As an older feminist thinker, Janet Radcliffe Richards, has put it: 'It is too dangerous to try to "free" women who are regarded as conditioned by forcing them to do what prevailing feminist ideology presumes they must want, because with that method there is always the danger of ignoring women's real wishes. They may not be conditioned at all'.[43]

A different 'phenomenological' perspective on these issues is provided by an American feminist and nurse, Margarete Sandelowski.[44] Basing her observations on interview data with

101

infertile women, Sandelowski describes the painfully ambivalent position of such women vis-à-vis the feminist movement. As noted before, they are judged by some feminists to be victims of false consciousness and of being self-interestedly dismissive of the common good of women. Sandelowski replies to these charges by emphasising the legitimacy of individual women's experience of infertility and of their desires to have children with the assistance of technology:

> The infertile woman, here and now, forces those of us who care for her to deal with a distinctively feminist moral dilemma: how to engage an individual woman's concrete situation in its immediacy while engaging the condition of women as a social group. Feminists call for social rather than individual solutions to the problem that technological and other controversial solutions (such as surrogacy) for infertility pose for women and for feminist theory and action, but infertility itself is experienced individually ... The first social solution to the problem with no nice feminist answer is for feminists neither to minimize the painful reality of infertility nor to trivialize the desire to conceive and bear a child. We do not have to deny the infertile woman's agency to be vigilant of the consequences for women of technological developments in reproduction. We do not have to question the infertile woman's right to choose the solutions to infertility available to her to affirm any woman's right to reproductive freedom. We do not have to suspect the infertile woman's desire for a child of her 'own' (genetically, gestationally), or a child who might have been her own, to celebrate the value of all children or to protect birth mothers from being forced to relinquish their children. We do have to make a comfortable place for her at the center of our passionate debates.[45]

Social and legal implications

The implications of this discussion of the various new forms of procreation and family formation are obvious enough. First, in a liberal society the 'right to procreative liberty', with all that it entails, should be recognised and legislative prohibitions should be removed. (That does not mean, as we have seen, that the state has no right to regulate the alternative forms of family formation in much the same way as adoption is regulated.) This is particularly the case with surrogate motherhood. If it is not the business of the state to force or coerce a woman to have a child, by making abortion illegal, it is equally not the business of the state to prevent a woman from having a child by whatever means she chooses. (Could a woman or a man choose then to have a child through an incestuous relationship? Leaving aside moral and religious objections to incest, insofar as there is a real risk that the legalisation of incest would lead to the harmful exploitation by one family member of another, relatively defenceless member, the answer is no.)

Second, in a liberal society access to the new forms of reproductive technology should be open to all and restrictions on access — for example, limiting IVF to legally married couples — should be removed. People exercising their right to procreative liberty in alternative ways should not be in any worse position than those in a traditional married situation. At present in many countries people seeking to overcome their infertility by IVF are restricted in all kinds of ways that married and fertile people would never tolerate. For example, under some legislation they have to prove their moral fitness to have children as well as satisfying stringent personal (age, for instance) and medical tests. Most people in ordinary marriage situations would feel affronted if they were forced to pass such tests before they were 'allowed' by the state to have children. However, some are quite prepared to treat infertile women and couples in this illiberal way.

Finally, as a corollary of the above, access to adequate health resources should be made possible for all. If the state recognises the family as a central social institution it should be prepared to fund alternative forms of family formation in the same way as it funds traditional forms. It cannot, in justice, discriminate against the infertile and those who choose alternative means of procreation.

Bioethics in a liberal society

NOTES

1. Joseph Raz, *The Morality of Freedom*, Oxford, Clarendon Press, 1986, pp.392–3.
2. J.A. Robertson, 'Embryos, families and procreative liberty: the legal structure of the new reproduction', *Southern California Law Review*, 59, 1986, pp.939–1041.
3. Lisa C. Ikemoto, 'Providing protection for collaborative, noncoital reproduction: surrogate motherhood and other new procreative technologies, and the right of intimate association', *Rutgers Law Review*, 4, 1988, pp.302–3.
4. *Access to Reproductive Technology*, Adelaide, National Bioethics Consultative Committee, 1990.
5. Linda and Maggie Kirkman, *My Sister's Child*, Melbourne, Penguin Books, 1988.
6. *Access to Reproductive Technology*, op. cit., p.3.
7. Ruth Macklin, 'Artificial means of reproduction and our understanding of the family', *Hastings Center Report*, 21, 1991, pp.5–11.
8. Nancy E. Reame and Philip J. Parker, 'Surrogate pregnancy; clinical features of forty four cases', *American Journal of Obstetrics and Gynecology*, 162, 199, p.1222.
9. *IVF and GIFT Pregnancies in Australia and New Zealand, 1988*, National Perinatal Statistics Unit, University of Sydney, 1990.
10. Verspieren bases his own reservations about artificial insemination on other grounds. Patrick Verspieren, 'Moralité de l'insémination artificielle', *Etudes*, 363, 1985, p.489.
11. Lynda Birke, Susan Himmelweit and Gail Vines, *Tomorrow's Child. Reproductive Technologies in the 90s*, London, Virago, 1990, p.19.
12. Report on surrogacy by the Anglican Social Responsibilities Committee of the Archdiocese of Melbourne, Australia, 1990.
13. Brent Parker Smith, 'Anna J. v. Mark C.: proof of the imminent need for surrogate motherhood regulation', *Journal of Family Law*, 13, 1991–2, p.495.
14. See *Australian Family Law Act 1975*, s60 D. See also Stephanie Charlesworth, J. Neville Turner and Lynne Foreman, *Lawyers, Social workers and Families*, Annandale, The Federation Press, 1990, pp.90–2.
15. Laura M. Purdy, 'Surrogate mothering: exploitation or empowerment?', *Bioethics*, 3, 1989, 31.
16. Colin D. Matthews in *Surrogacy: Biomedical Dilemmas in the 1990s*, Adelaide, Dietrich Bonhoeffer International Institute for Bioethical Studies, 1990, p.4.

17. Carol Gilligan, *In a Different Voice: Psychological Theory and Women's Development*, Cambridge, Mass., Harvard University Press, 1982.
18. Lynda Birke, Susan Himmelweit and Gail Vines, *Tomorrow's Child: Reproductive Technology in the 1990s*, op. cit., pp.3–4.
19. ibid., p.4.
20. Carol Gilligan, *In a Different Voice*, op. cit., p.166.
21. Shulamith Firestone, *The Dialectic of Sex*, London, Jonathan Cape, 1971.
22. Mara Mies, 'Do we need all this? A call against genetic engineering and reproductive technology', in Patricia Spallone and Deborah Steinberg (eds.), *Made to Order: The Myth of Reproductive and Genetic Progress*, New York, Oxford University Press, 1987.
23. Gena Corea, *The Mother Machine*, New York, Harper and Row, 1982, p.39.
24. Christine Overall, *Ethics and Human Reproduction*, London, Allen and Unwin, 1983.
25. ibid., p.125.
26. Susan Dodds and Karen Jones, 'Surrogacy and autonomy', *Bioethics*, 3, 1989, p.13.
27. ibid., p.17.
28. Heather Dietrich, Dissenting View, *Surrogacy Report*, National Bioethics Consultative Committee, 1990, p.62.
29. Robyn Rowland, 'Making women visible in the embryo experimentation debate', *Bioethics*, 1, 1987, p.5.
30. Karen Dawson, *Human Embryo Experimentation: A Background Paper and Select Bibliography*, National Bioethics Consultative Committee, 1990, p.32. This is not Dawson's own position.
31. Lynda Birke, Susan Himmelweit and Gail Vines, *Tomorrow's Child*, op. cit., p.x.
32. Mary Anne Warren, 'IVF and women's interests', *Bioethics*, 2, 1988, p.53.
33. ibid., p.54.
34. Christine Overall, 'Surrogate mothering: exploitation or empowerment?', *Bioethics*, 3, 1989, p.24.
35. Lisa C. Ikemoto, 'Providing protection for collaborative, noncoital reproduction', pp.302–3.
36. Sharyn L. Roach Anleu, 'Reinforcing gender norms: commercial and altruistic surrogacy', *Acta Sociologica*, 33, 1990, p.70.
37. ibid., p.72.
38. Lynda Birke, Susan Himmelweit and Gail Vines, *Tomorrow's Child*, op. cit., pp.266–7.
39. ibid.

40. Karen Dawson and Beth Gaze, 'Who is the subject of the research?', in Peter Singer *et al.* (eds.), *Embryo Experimentation*, Melbourne, Cambridge University Press, 1990.
41. Mary Anne Warren, in Peter Singer *et al.* (eds.), *Embryo Experimentation*, op. cit., pp.125–40.
42. Mary Anne Warren, 'A Reply to Holmes on Gendercide', *Bioethics*, 1, 1987, p.198. See also Warren's book, *Gendercide: The Implications of Sex Selection*, New Jersey, Rowman and Allanheld, 1985. See also Marlene Gerber Fried (ed.), *From Abortion to Reproductive Freedom: Transforming a Movement*, Boston, South End Press, 1990, especially the essay by Kathryn Kolbert, 'Developing a Reproductive Rights Agenda for the 1990s'.
43. Janet Radcliffe Richards, *The Sceptical Feminist*, Harmondsworth, Penguin, 1982, p.113.
44. Margarete Sandelowski, 'Fault lines: infertility and imperilled sisterhood', *Feminist Studies*, 16, 1990, pp.33–51.
45. ibid., p.48.

5

Distributing Health-care Resources

The problem of scarce resources

The problem of how health-care resources should be allocated or apportioned, so that they are distributed in both the most just and most efficient way, is not a new one. Every health system in an economically developed society is faced with the need to decide (either informally or formally) what proportion of the community's total resources should be spent on health care; how resources are to be apportioned; which human diseases and disabilities and which forms of treatment are to be given priority; which members of the community are to be given special consideration in respect of their health needs; and which forms of treatment are the most cost-effective.

What is new is that from the 1950s onwards there have been certain general changes in outlook about the finitude of resources as a whole and of health-care resources in particular, as well as more specific changes regarding the clientele of health-care resources and the cost to the community of those resources. Thus in the 1950s and 1960s there emerged an awareness in Western societies that resources for the provision of fossil fuel energy were finite and exhaustible and that the capacity of nature or the environment to sustain economic development and population was also finite. In other words, we became aware of the obvious fact that there were 'limits to growth'. The new consciousness that there were also severe limits to health-care resources was part of this general revelation of the obvious. Looking back, it now seems quite incredible that in the national health systems that emerged in many countries after the Second World War it was assumed without question that all the basic health needs of any community could be satisfied, at least in principle. God, or the 'invisible hand' of economic progress, would provide.

However, exactly at the same time as this new realisation of the finite character of health-care resources was sinking in, an awareness of a contrary kind was developing in Western societies: that people have a basic right to health care as a necessary condition of a properly human life. Like education, political and legal processes and institutions, public order, communication, transport and money supply, health care came to be seen as one of the fundamental social facilities necessary for people to exercise their other rights as autonomous human beings. People are not in a position to exercise personal liberty and to be self-determining if they are poverty stricken, or deprived of basic education, or do not live within a context of law and order. In the same way, basic health care is a condition of the exercise of autonomy.

Although the language of 'rights' sometimes leads to confusion, it is now recognised in most societies that people have a right to health care (though there has been some resistance in the US to the idea that there is a formal right to health care). It is also accepted that this right generates an obligation or duty for the state to ensure that adequate health care is provided and that there should be equal access to whatever health-care resources are provided out of the public purse. The state has no obligation to provide a health-care system itself, but to ensure that such a system is provided. Put in another way, basic health care is now recognised as a 'public good' rather than a 'private good' that one is expected to buy for oneself. As the 1976 declaration of the

World Health Organisation put it: 'The enjoyment of the highest attainable standard of health is one of the fundamental rights of every human being without distinction of race, religion, political belief, economic or social condition'.[1] As has just been re-marked, in a liberal society basic health is seen as one of the indispensable conditions for the exercise of personal autonomy.

Just at the time then when it became obvious that health-care resources could not possibly meet the demands being made upon them, people were demanding that their fundamental right to health care be satisfied by the state.

The second set of more specific changes that have led to the present concern about the distribution of health-care resources stems from the dramatic rise in health costs in most developed countries, accompanied by large-scale demographic and social changes which have meant, to take one example, that elderly people are now major (and relatively very expensive) con-sumers of health-care resources. Thus in OECD countries as a whole, health costs increased from 3.8 per cent of GDP in 1960 to 7 per cent of GDP in 1980, and it has been predicted that the proportion of health costs to GDP will continue to increase. (In the US the current figure is about 12 per cent of GDP and in Australia about 7.8 per cent of GDP.)

As a consequence, during the 1980s a kind of neo-Malthusian doomsday scenario (analogous to similar doomsday extrapol-ations about energy needs and fossil fuels or about population increases) was projected by health administrators, economists and politicians. In this scenario ever-rising health costs were matched against static or declining resources, since it was as-sumed that the community would not tolerate more than 10 per cent of GDP being spent on health care. (It should be remarked that both the doomsday scenario and the assumption that some-thing like 10 per cent of GDP is the absolute limit have been called critically into question. As it has been argued: 'If the WHO dec-laration claiming a universal human right to health is to have any substance beyond its obvious manifesto content, the only way to back it up nationally as well as internationally is a thorough re-evaluation of public budgetary allocations'.)[2] At the same time it has become clear to all except 'free market' ideologues that a market-based health-care system does not offer a solution to this rapidly escalating problem. Thus it has been pointed out that:

> in the 1980s, while other Western countries constrained expenditures, the so-called 'competition revolution' in the United States was associated with an increase in the rate at which health costs have been increasing ... Apart from its generally unacceptable distributional effects the unregulated market does not appear to allocate health care resources efficiently. Market-based systems may prove to be viable if an appropriate regulatory framework can be devised, but any system must face the apparently inescapable fact that consumers will not be the agents that decide between the technical alternatives.[3]

Or, as another critic has put it:

> The market ideology fails in health care quite simply because the market fails in health care. That failure is fundamental. Markets cannot work adequately without informed consumers. Patients in many consumption decisions in health care are not informed or at least not sufficiently so. Indeed, often what they consume is information.[4]

In this general context the debate over the allocation of health-care resources has been mainly about economic evaluation and efficient rationing of those resources on a costs and benefits basis. As a result, the specifically ethical dimensions of the debate have tended to be neglected. It seems to have been assumed that if we can devise acceptable forms of cost–benefit rationing of health-care resources the ethical questions can be left to look after themselves.

This assumption, however, is both wrong-headed and dangerous since the allocation of health-care resources is not merely a matter of efficient cost–benefit rationing but above all a matter of human justice or equity where the interests of all concerned — patients, health-care professionals, the community at large —

have to be given their due. Again, as we shall see, the value of personal autonomy also plays a central part, in that in a liberal society people should as far as possible have real alternatives and choices in health care and also a real degree of control over the deployment of health resources. A paternalistic system of the old kind where medical professionals effectively controlled health care, and paternalism of the new kind where health economists, policy planners and bureaucrats are increasingly controlling health care in the name of 'rational' cost-effective planning, cannot be squared with the values of a liberal society.

More generally, the allocation of health care resources is a business where ethical values play a part at every level of the allocation process — governmental, bureaucratic, institutional, clinical unit, individual patient. It might also be added that different kinds of ethical issues arise at the different levels. Thus the kinds of ethical questions that emerge at the clinical level are quite unlike those that arise at the institutional or hospital level. As Aristotle noted some time ago, the concept of 'health' is not a univocal one which has the same meaning in all of its applications but a much looser one which has a varying or 'analogous' meaning. The same is true of the concept of 'health care'.

Utilitarian approaches

As we shall see, the debate about the distribution of health-care resources has been dominated by a consequentialist or utilitarian approach and method which determines the value of medical treatment, health-care policies or strategies exclusively in terms of measurable consequences or 'outcomes'. Utilitarianism is a protean concept but it is taken here to be a species of consequentialism in that it is concerned with (a) general welfare or happiness, or satisfaction of preferences or wants, as a consequence of our acts, and (b) with consequences that are quantifiable and summable in the sense that we can add together the welfare, happiness or satisfaction of many different people

111

affected by our acts. Thus, for example, if five people are made happier by act X as against one person being made happy by act Y, then act X is five times better than act Y.

At a time when in mainstream theoretical ethics utilitarianism has been stringently criticised and is now in considerable disarray as an ethical theory,[5] it has become the darling of the health-care resource allocation experts. The late Cambridge philosopher C.D. Broad once remarked that all good philosophical heresies go to America when they die, but whether or not that is true, utilitarianism has certainly found a home among health-care economists, planners and bureaucrats, even if it has fallen out of favour with many professional moral philosophers.

Utilitarian approaches in health-care resource allocation are basically concerned with getting the best outcomes for health dollars spent and there is of course nothing wrong with that laudable aim so long as it is concerned with means to already decided ends or goals, and not with the determination of the ends or goals themselves. (For example, we cannot plausibly show, on utilitarian premises, that we should respect the lives of gravely disabled newborn infants. But given that we have decided, on non-utilitarian grounds, that we should respect the lives of disabled newborns, we can show which are the most effective ways of expressing that respect in a given set of circumstances.) But at the same time utilitarianism lends itself to a form of bureaucratic and 'expert' paternalism which is impatient with the liberal ideal of individual autonomy and other connected liberal values, such as the provision of diversity of choice. As it has been put: in a liberal society 'the government has an obligation to create an environment providing individuals with an adequate range of options and the opportunities to choose them'.[6] But for the utilitarian an *efficient and effective* health system is a *good* health system regardless of whether the health choices of individuals are diminished or not. (It might be argued that utilitarianism could accommodate itself to the goal of enlargement of choice in this area in that a good health strategy would be one which had the consequence or outcome of maximising autonomy and choice in the most cost-effective way. But, as we shall see, it is not possible to quantify and measure and do sums about such a consequence or outcome [greater autonomy] in the way required by the theory of utilitarianism.)

Utilitarianism has always found it difficult to cope with the idea of personal autonomy as an ethical value. (The great exemplar of classical utilitarianism was Bentham's Panopticon, the quintessentially efficient prison system which allowed total surveillance of the prisoners without a thought for them as human beings.) As Rawls argues, for the utilitarian,

> in calculating the greatest balance of satisfaction it does not matter, except indirectly, what the desires are for. We are to arrange institutions so as to obtain the greatest sum of satisfaction: we ask no questions about their source or quality, but only how their satisfaction would affect the total of well-being ... Thus if men take a certain pleasure in discriminating against one another, in subjecting others to a lesser liberty as a means of enhancing their self-respect, then the satisfaction of their desires must be weighed in our deliberations according to their interests, or whatever, along with other desires.[7]

Rawls goes on to argue that utilitarianism cannot provide a basis for personal self-respect.[8]

Mill pretends that autonomy, liberty and individuality are based upon 'the principle of utility', but in fact the values of autonomy and personal liberty are for him as absolute as they are for Kant. They are intrinsic goods regardless of any consequences they may have and there is, for Mill, no envisageable set of circumstances in which the general recognition of autonomy and liberty might have such untoward consequences that their restriction would be justified. As remarked before, there is in fact no necessary link between utilitarianism and liberalism.

One can understand why the utilitarian approach is so seductive for politicians and health-care economists and planners when there is a relative scarcity of health-care resources and hard choices have to be made. The great attraction of classical utilitarianism as an ethical theory was that it appeared to offer a rational and hard-headed way of solving just such ethical problems. In principle, as we have seen, for the utilitarian the outcomes or consequences of an act or policy are quantifiable and measurable; as such they can be measured against and compared with outcomes of alternative acts or policies and one can calculate which is the better. In practice these measurements, comparisons and calculations may be very difficult to make, but in principle — the utilitarian holds — they can always be made. It is this act of faith that, as we have said, makes utilitarianism as a theory attractive to many people who are faced with having to make difficult ethical decisions.

A corollary of this view is that, once again in principle, we are never really faced with irresolvable ethical conflicts or dilemmas where two ethical principles come into collision with each other, as for example in abortion when the mother's right to control her own reproductive processes comes into conflict with the fetus's quasi-right to live (given that it is a developing organism which, if all goes well, will eventually become a human being). For the utilitarian there cannot be an irreducible plurality of human goods that are not able in principle to be compared with and weighed against each other and a solution 'calculated'. That would be an 'irrational' situation.

It is not difficult to show that all of these assumptions of utilitarianism are open to serious objections and that the appearance of hard-nosed rationalism is illusory. All human acts or policies have consequences or outcomes but most of them do not have *quantifiable and measurable* outcomes with a dollar sign in front of them, which can be compared with and measured against other acts and policies, and calculated as being 'better' or 'worse' than the latter. Being in love, writing poetry, doing philosophy, engaging in scientific investigations all have consequences or outcomes and we can tell in a general way whether or not we have been successful in those activities. But none have *quantifiably measurable* outcomes which enable us to compare them with each other. We cannot say that being in love is 'better' or 'worse' than doing philosophy. They are irreducible human goods which cannot be measured in a quantifiable way and weighed against each other. In the same way, the primary values assumed in health-care resource allocation are non-utilitarian values or 'intrinsic goods' which cannot be measured, compared and calculated. And a corollary of this is that ethical dilemmas or conflicts in this area are always possible.

However, the fact that ethical values do not obey the rules of utilitarian cost–benefit 'rationality' does not mean that they are thereby 'irrational' and that we cannot meaningfully say whether a medical policy is just or unjust; or whether it is paternalistic or respects personal autonomy; or whether a hospital system is more or less beneficent or compassionate. One gets the impression from some of the health-care utilitarians that only since the recent arrival of cost-effective measurement procedures have we been able to say whether a health system or policy is successful or not. Previously, they imply, we blundered about in total darkness, trusting our intuitions and hunches, but not really knowing what the real consequences or outcomes were and thus whether or not what we were doing was worthwhile.

The moral of all this is that, while there is a wholly legitimate place for a utilitarian outcomes approach in the distribution of health-care resources at the level of means, there are also central non-utilitarian values and outcomes that cannot be measured in a cost–benefit way, though that is not to say that we cannot judge them rationally. As Plato and Aristotle reminded us a long time ago, there are non-utilitarian forms of rationality.

Justice (or equity or fairness) is closely linked with autonomy since it is concerned with treating people with equal respect precisely because they are autonomous moral agents or persons. To discriminate against people because of their race, colour, gender or age is unjust because these characteristics have nothing directly to do with a person's status as a self-determining moral agent. If it could be shown that a person's race, colour, gender, age or social class in some way made them less of a moral agent in the full sense, then discrimination would not be unjust. In the past, of course, people have tried to show that race, colour and gender do in fact make a difference to a person's status as a moral agent. Aristotle, for example, held that slaves were not fully human and were not capable of autonomous action; colonialist powers took much the same view of the indigenous peoples they colonised, and medieval Christian theologians claimed that women could not be ordained priests because they were in a state of 'subjection' or inferiority — in other words, they were not fully autonomous agents. The pretence was that these people were in the state of moral immaturity Mill speaks about when he says that his doctrine does not apply to children nor to people in 'those backward states of society in which the race itself may be considered as in its nonage'.[9] Similarly in Australia the indigenous Australian Aborigines were held by the white invaders not to be capable of owning land, so that the entire Australian continent was declared to be *terra nullius* and the English settlers were thereby legally able to appropriate the Aborigines' lands. We now, of course, reject those attempts to single out various groups as being of diminished autonomy and too morally immature to be considered in an equal way with other people and to be accorded equal respect.

Utilitarianism has not been able to provide a plausible account of distributive justice. For the utilitarian a just act or policy is one which produces, on balance, quantifiably greater benefits for the maximum number of people. It may be that a minority of people are gravely disadvantaged by the policy but these disadvantages or costs are outweighed by the benefits to the majority. The policy is therefore 'just' even if the minority is treated in a discriminatory or partial way (as though they were not fully autonomous and not worthy of the respect due to autonomous agents or persons). Mill speaks of the 'tyranny of the majority' which occurs when the majority unjustly uses its power to secure its advantage at the expense of the minority, but he doesn't seem to see that this kind of 'tyranny' is a necessary feature of utilitarian and majoritarian 'justice'. As many critics have pointed out, utilitarianism cannot provide an ethical basis for protecting the interests of minorities and powerless groups. 'The utilitarian strategy', an American philosopher argues, 'does not take into account the distribution of benefits and harms. It merely examines net aggregate benefits, which implies that if enough people receive the benefits, it is plausible that even more enormous harms to a small number will be outweighed by the aggregate benefit to the masses'.[10]

Of course, in practical affairs we have to use various devices to get agreements so that decisions can be made. The will of the majority is one of those devices, but there is nothing mystical or sacred about majority votes and decisions. 'Vox populi' is not really 'vox Dei' and the morality of acts and policies cannot be determined by an appeal to majority wishes or preferences.

A health system in a liberal society

What requirements does the liberal society demand of a health system? Or, put in another way, given the values of personal autonomy and of justice, what kind of health-care system and what priorities for the allocation of health-care resources are indicated?

We must first provide a rough definition of 'health care' since, as we shall see, its meaning is not at all clear and distinct. Many discussions about the allocation of health resources assume without question that health care can be defined as that care which professional and institutional (and technological) medicine can provide. As Hafdan Mahler, former director-general of the World Health Organisation, once put it: 'Everywhere it appears that health workers consider that the "best" health care is one where everything known to medicine is applied to every individual, by the highest trained medical scientist, in the most specialised institution'.[11] As against this 'medicalisation' of health care, WHO's 'Health For All' strategy has emphasised the interdependence between health and socio-economic development and the importance of primary care: that is, people's awareness of and response to their own health problems and a recognition that health care is dependent upon housing, water purity and supply, transport, mass media, communications and so on. Again, emphasis is placed on issues of social justice and social power. 'The "new public health" ', it has been said, 'goes beyond the conventional paradigm of illness as the outcome of the assaults of pathogens, poor nutrition, addictions, unhygienic living conditions or genetic predisposition, to address the contribution of social justice, social action, power and access to resources to shaping people's health and life chances'.[12]

The public health movement has largely emphasised three issues: rearranging social factors to prevent disease and illness, sharing resources for the prevention of illness and curative medicine as equitably as possible, engaging likely sufferers in preventive medicine and in managing their own treatment. In general the movement has emphasised prevention and care as against medical intervention and cure. It is obvious that the allocation of health resources in this context is very different from that in the context of specific medical resources and that the ethical issues involved are also very different. For example,

> effective implementation of WHO's 'Health for All' might require expenditure upon a health policy impact unit or a statistical collection unit. Which would achieve the greater good? If the latter, what weight should be given to privacy considerations against notions of the public good.[13]

Hicks complains that ethical issues raised by public health have been given little attention by health ethicists: 'The Encyclopedia of Bioethics gives about 5 per cent of its space to public health questions — a proportion, ironically, roughly analogous to the balance between medicine and public health spending in the US'. And he goes on to argue:

> A public health ethics approach would regard good health questions as a sub-set of 'good life' questions. Therefore it would ask whether banning the advertising of alcohol would be justified by the risk it posed to free speech or whether a punitive approach to the AIDS epidemic would be worth the damage it would do to that toleration of difference which is a good test of the richness of texture of the society.[14]

It has also been claimed that health promotion, which is an essential part of public health, is often neglected in debates about health-care resources because it is not easy to measure it in economic terms. 'Health promotion offers benefits for the distant future, which it is standard for economists to discount. Moreover, structural health promotion, which is the basis of the New Public Health promulgated by the World Health Organisation, is a risky field in which it is usually impossible to predict or measure the health benefits which accrue from individual programs'.[15] In addition a good deal of health-care resource allocation takes place in a disguised or surreptitious form in other areas such as education, the alleviation of poverty and housing. By and large, in the health-care field the rich and well-to-do fare better and the poor fare worse: 'People with the least education, people who live in the least desirable neighbourhoods, and people who work at the least prestigious jobs are all more likely to die earlier than people at the other end of these scales . . . virtually every disease strikes the lowest class more heavily'.[16] The upshot of all this is that 'health care' and 'health-care resources' are diffuse and ill-defined concepts. If, as has been said, improved education may have, in certain circumstances, a long-term effect on improving the health of a community, then education is a health-care 'resource'. This, of course, makes any resource allocation scheme very difficult to run.

Patient and physician

Within the area of medical health care, the relationship between the patient and the physician and other health professionals and institutions is of course crucial to the debate about the allocation of resources. We have already touched on this issue and noted how difficult it is to find an appropriate model for the relationship. We need to find a middle way between the older and newer forms of medical paternalism which diminish the personal autonomy of the patient, and on the other hand the view that patients should be in full control of their medical treatment with the physician being a mere servant.

The patient, it is true, has the primary responsibility for her or his own health care and can accept or refuse medical treatment. The physician must respect the patient's autonomy and right of self-determination in this respect: that is the basis of the essential requirement of informed consent to medical treatment. On the other hand the autonomy of the physician and other health professionals also has to be taken into account and their role cannot be reduced to that of servants. In many cases the patient must rely upon and trust in the professional knowledge and technical competence of the physician. And the physician may have to do what he or she judges to be for the good of the patient where the patient is not able or competent to consent to the treatment and to exercise some degree of control over it.

From this point of view the American health ethicist Daniel Callahan has questioned the notion of 'patient rights'.

If we want to have good doctor–patient relationships, we can't reduce that relationship exclusively to the language of rights, particularly the language of patient rights. A consequence is to jeopardise the doctor's important role as a moral agent. At one extreme the doctor is turned into nothing but a plumber. The challenge is to recognise that when doctors and patients enter into a relationship they begin to create a community, or at least a profound relationship which the language of rights does not adequately describe. In one sense each has to help the other. The doctor has to educate the patient, help the patient understand what might serve his or her welfare. And the patient has to find a way to tell the physician what he or she is trying to live for. It ought to be a richer language than is captured in the language of autonomy and rights.[17]

There is, no doubt, something to be said for Callahan's view: but far from demonstrating the need to go beyond the language of autonomy and rights it reinforces the centrality of that language, in that the physician–patient relationship involves each in mutual respect for the autonomy of the other. The physician must respect the patient's autonomous right to control his or her own health and to refuse treatment (even if death ensues) and to demand the right to exercise informed consent; the patient must respect the physician's right as a professional to insist upon professional standards and to exercise some degree of justified paternalism where the patient cannot, or is unwilling to, take responsibility for his or her own health-care decisions.

There is an analogy between the patient–physician relationship and the relationship between learner and teacher, since in both cases the physician and teacher are (ideally) *enabling* the patient and student to assume responsibility for their own health and learning respectively. One cannot *cause* or determine another to be an autonomous or self-determining agent — that would be a contradiction in terms — but one can nevertheless create conditions which enable others to awaken to the meaning of their autonomy and the realisation that they are masters of their fate and captains of their own souls. Knowing is an autonomous act which people must do for themselves, but teachers can, like a Socratic midwife, help students to be no longer faithful parrots but to know and understand for themselves. In the same way the physician must always, so far as is possible, help patients to exercise some degree of autonomous control over their health. That means that patients, like student learners, must have genuine choices and alternatives available to them.

Where incompetent or unwilling patients are concerned, medical paternalism always has to be justified and the onus of justification is always on the one practising paternalism. As we noted, the test must always be: is this something which the patient, were she fully informed and fully competent, would clearly consent to herself? Even here the physician must have respect for the autonomy of the patient.

In the present context, when so much emphasis is placed upon the scarcity of health-care resources, physicians and other health professionals are being asked to consider the social dimensions of health care. Some critics have complained that the rational allocation of health-care resources will never be possible so long as physicians do not take account of the larger social need to ration resources but remain fixated myopically on the needs of the particular patient in front of them. But in a very real sense physicians and other health carers must remain committed to using their professional skills to meet the health-care needs of the individual patient. No doubt the physician must operate within certain given economic and other constraints, but it is not his or her business, as a physician, to act as a gatekeeper and to control access to health-care resources. There is a confusion of aims and functions if health-care professionals have both to work for the good of the patient before them and to be committed to the primacy of the needs of that patient, and at the same time are required to act as cost-containment experts on behalf of the health system and the community.

On the other hand, it has been argued that while the two roles are in principle distinct the physician has willy nilly to combine both in practice. Thus the US medical ethicist Edmund Pellegrino has written:

> In these matters, the physician serves best as an expert witness, providing the basis for informed public decisions. He must lead in pointing out deficiencies and raising the painful matter of choices. At the same time each doctor must honor his traditional contract to his own patient. He cannot allow the larger social issues to undermine that solicitude. The ethically responsive doctor will thus find himself more and more involved in social and individual ethical values, impelled to act responsibly in both spheres. The Hippocratic ethic and its later modifications were not required to confront such

paradoxes. Today's conscientious physician is very much in need of an expanded ethic to cope with his double responsibility to the individual and to the community.[18]

Health-care resource allocations: four examples

These then are the most general features that a health system in a liberal society should have. However, it is worthwhile examining in a little detail how ethical considerations arise in specific and concrete areas of health-care resource allocation. A major difficulty here is that the different levels of decision-making are usually not distinguished from one another. Decisions at the level of governmental policy-makers and health bureaucrats, who have to allocate health-care resources in competition with other areas — such as defence, education, law — are made in a very different way (and have different ethical implications) from the decisions made by hospital administrators who have to divide up a given health budget between the competing departments of a hospital. And within a given department or unit, such as an intensive care unit for newborns, very particular and immediate decisions have to be made about the allocation of resources to competing kinds of patients, for example 500 gram birthweight infants as against 1000 gram birthweight infants. The ethical issues that arise at this level are very different from those facing the hospital administrator or the health bureaucrat. Again, at the individual physician–patient level, ethical questions present themselves in a more subtle way. As we shall see, there is a complex array of ethical values, sometimes concordant sometimes discordant, involved in making decisions in these areas. These values set severe limits to 'rational' planning of a utilitarian cost–benefit kind.

Access to reproductive technology

Most people acknowledge that infertility is a disability and that people who are infertile should have access to certain forms of medical treatment (tubal surgery, hormonal treatment, sperm analysis and the like). But there is strong disagreement about how *serious* a disability infertility is and how great a claim treatment for infertility has upon publicly provided health-care resources, and whether such treatment should be seen as part of the 'basic health care' which is supposed to be available to all.

Some people see infertility as a grave disability, both psychologically and socially. A disability or a disease is not merely a bodily dysfunction, but a bodily dysfunction *in a given social context*. Thus infertility prevents people doing what other people in their circumstances are usually or normally able to do. Those who hold that infertility is a serious disability point to the high value given to the family in our society and to the fact that infertility prevents family formation. If the family is so important, they argue, then one would think that infertile couples would have a strong claim on health-care resources so as to enable them, as far as is feasible, to form a family.

It has been estimated (although no firm evidence is available) that the incidence of infertility in Australia is of the order of 8–10 per cent. With regard to the various forms of artificial procreation used to alleviate infertility, some 5000–6000 donor inseminations are carried out in Australia each year; it is estimated that there is a 10–15 per cent chance of conception in an insemination cycle and the live birth rate is thought to be 6–10 per cent per cycle. In addition there were, in 1988, some 9000 *in vitro* fertilisation cycles carried out in Australia and New Zealand, of which 743 or 8.1 per cent resulted in a live birth. Again, there were 2800 GIFT (gamete intrafallopian transfer) treatment cycles carried out, of which 528 or 18.4 per cent resulted in a live birth. The number of people seeking alleviation of their infertility through these treatments is therefore considerable and, given the rigours of the treatments they have to undergo, one could say that they see the having of a child through IVF or GIFT, and thus the formation of a family, as of at least as much value to them as most other treatments for non life-threatening health conditions. It might be mentioned here that infertile couples do not claim, as is sometimes alleged, that they have a 'right' to have a child, any more than people generally claim to have a right to good health. What they claim is that they have a right of access to public health funds for the treatment of their condition in exactly the same way that other people have a right of access to funds and treatment for ill health or disease.

Others, however, as we have seen, view infertility as being relatively unimportant in itself. Women in our society, they say, are conditioned by the 'pro-natalist' culture to think that being a mother and bearing a child is necessary to their identity as women, so that one cannot be a 'real' woman unless one has had a child. But this is a form of 'false consciousness'. Women can be 'child free' and yet lead fulfilled lives.

> Having a child and forming a family may be very satisfying to some couples, but this is not a basic need, like education, which generates a 'right'. There are many things we would like to have, but cannot have, and we cannot claim that we have a 'right' to have them. Having children is one of those things.[19]

It is clear from what has been said that we cannot decide how health-care resources should be allocated to the alleviation of infertility by the various forms of reproductive technology unless we first settle the question of how we value infertility, that is determine how serious a human disability it is. That, as we have seen, is a complex business since we are dealing not just with a bodily dysfunction but with a dysfunction with a social aspect: how infertility is perceived within a particular socio-cultural context.

If we are able to decide upon a valuation of infertility and its alleviation by reproductive technology we then have to decide whether IVF and GIFT are efficient means of alleviation, and how they are to be ranked against other alternative services. In one sense the success rate is not very good (this is especially true of IVF). But (a) it is much better than zero since there are at present no other alternatives; (b) given the medical history of the infertile patients presenting for IVF treatment it is to be expected that success rates will be low; (c) it is claimed that it is not far short of mother nature's own success rate in that a high percentage of naturally formed embryos *in utero* do not implant or are spontaneously aborted; and (d) there are good prospects of improved success rates resulting from further research.[20]

Regarding costs, the estimated costs for 5000 couples on IVF programs in 1987 in Australia was some $30 million, of which the federal government paid $17 million, the patients $6 million and health insurance funds $7 million. It has been estimated that, all up, the cost of each IVF 'take home' baby is about $40 000. (Funding for IVF was changed in 1990 by the government's decision to extend funding for the various components of IVF treatment. This initiative suggested that, in the government's perception, IVF and the other forms of reproductive technology were now accepted by the community and that infertility was also seen as a sufficiently grave condition to warrant health-care funds being used to provide medical treatment to enable people to have children.)

Some have claimed that the costs of IVF treatment are disproportionately high. It is true that they appear so when compared with the costs of ordinary natural childbirth. But if they are compared with the costs of keeping a low-weight premature infant (born through natural childbirth) alive by intensive care, and of coping with the continuing effects of its premature birth, often through the rest of its life, then $40 000 per IVF child is very cheap. No one argues that intensive care for newborns should be restricted solely on the grounds that it is so costly and it is difficult to see why alleviation of infertility by IVF and GIFT, so that a child is able to be born, should be restricted solely for reasons of cost. (Though some have argued that intensive care 'saves' a life, whereas IVF 'merely' creates one, and that whereas we have an obligation in the first case we do not in the latter.)

What emerges from this discussion is the difficulty of deciding how health-care resources should be allocated to the alleviation of infertility by IVF and other forms of reproductive technology.

We must, in fact, rephrase the question to read: in the kind of society which has (a) opted for such and such a level of health-care services to be financed out of public funds and whose financial resources are at such and such a level; (b) where diseases and disabilities such as infertility are defined in such and such a way and given such and such a valuation ('serious', 'cosmetic' or whatever); (c) where there are very large differences about these valuations and health-care priorities among various groups in the community (for example, 'consumer groups' of infertile couples on IVF programs who see IVF as their only way of having a child and forming a family as against certain feminist groups which see IVF as 'male patriarchalist technology', and with a large number of people in between these two extremes) — what in this context is the fairest way of allocating health-care resources for the alleviation of infertility?

This complexity is further enhanced by the fact that these various groups continually engage in 'political' action to promote their own views and to bring about change in the prevailing situation regarding health-care resources for infertility. For example, vigorous lobbying by a US national infertility support group called 'Resolve' resulted in legislation defining infertility treatment, like pregnancy-related procedures, as medically necessary health benefits covered by insurance.[21] The same is true of IVF support groups in Australia. On the other hand there is a curious coalition of interests opposing IVF and reproductive technology in general, which comprises feminist groups such as FINRRAGE, conservative elements in the Catholic Church and anti-technology groups. Politicians and policy-makers have to take account of these lobbies since reproductive technology is now a contentious political issue in many countries.

Intensive care of newborns

In a sense the question of what value should be placed upon the intensive care of newborn infants is almost at the opposite extreme from that of the use of reproductive technology to

127

alleviate infertility. As we have seen, there are large differences in attitudes to the latter, but there is virtual unanimity about the high priority to be given to the intensive care of newborns. The principle of 'the sanctity of human life' has here its clearest application, and it is supported by the fact that newborn infants are seen as the most defenceless and vulnerable of all human beings. The powerful symbolism that attaches to the care of disabled newborns is a major factor in the way our community views such care. (One might contrast it with the much more ambivalent symbolic character of IVF: on the one hand it is seen as a way of bringing about 'the miracle of human birth', on the other hand it is seen as a way of 'playing God' and of attempting to technologise human reproduction.)

The costs of neonatal intensive care are, however, very high and vary in inverse proportion to the birthweight of the newborn infant.[22] For example, with regard to infants with a birthweight of 1000–1500 grams, the survival rate is 95 per cent and long-term neuro-developmental disability rates are only 5–10 per cent. The future quality of life of these infants is therefore, on average, very high. The average intensive care cost per surviving infant has been estimated at $22 199. When, however, infants with birthweights of less than 1000 grams are considered, the long-term survival rate is of the order of 60 per cent and the impairment rate is between 8 and 14 per cent. For infants with a birthweight of 900–999 grams the cost per survivor is $38 377. Overall, the average cost per survivor of infants of less than 800 grams birthweight is $128 409, while the cost per survivor of infants with a birthweight of more than 800 grams (800–899 grams) is $43 972. For infants with a birthweight between 500 and 599 grams the intensive care cost per survivor is $151 911.

Commenting on these costs, Tudehope *et al.* point to the pressures to institute a cut-off for intensive care at the 800 gram birthweight level, since it is there that the costs per survivor become so discrepant. Referring to 'expenses incurred with prolonged ventilatory care of infants who subsequently died', the authors say that in the intensive care unit of the Mater Misericordiae Mothers' Hospital in Brisbane, Australia, in 1987,

> four babies of birthweight 423 g, 626 g, 650 g, and 860 g, received mechanical ventilation for 102, 220, 126 and 112 days, respectively, at a cost of $691 408 for no survival. Had these babies been identified earlier as having no long-term future and ventilatory care terminated or not instituted, the cost per survivor of infants of birthweight under 1000 g in 1987, would have been reduced from $76 798 to $48 902. Although long-term survival at the Mater Hospital for infants of birthweight less than 1000 g has steadily improved from 31 per cent in 1977 to 62 per cent in 1987, there has been a concomitant increase in time for non-survivors.[23]

'There is a clear demarcation of costs of care', Tudehope *et al.* go on, 'for infants below 800 g compared with those above this limit. It could therefore be argued on utilitarian cost–benefit grounds that a birthweight of 800 g should be the cut-off level for non-introduction of neonatal intensive care because the cost of $128 409 per survivor below 800 g compared with the $43 972 per survivor between 800–999 g is too great a financial burden to society'.[24] The authors, however, reject this argument and say that 'such decisions should be based upon human compassion not upon economic expediency'.[25] They claim that economic considerations cannot by themselves be used to determine what amount of health-care resources should be allocated to this area. Neonatal intensive care costs, they argue, compare favourably with other expensive health treatments, such as coronary bypass surgery. For example, renal transplants cost $15 000 for the first year and $2000–2500 for the following ten years; renal dialysis costs $15 000–30 000 per year; liver transplants cost $60 000 per person; the total lifetime cost for each AIDS diagnosed patient is about $934 000 ($55 000 in direct health costs, including AZT, and $879 000 in indirect costs). Again, in terms of life years gained by each patient a newborn might gain up to 70 years (with 40 years as an economic contributor and taxpayer) as against an adult who might gain 15 years of productive life through coronary bypass surgery. Further, restricting individual high-cost medical treatments such as those involved in intensive care may be less economical than making savings in relatively low-cost but commonly used treatments with large clienteles.

As against arguments of economic expediency, Tudehope and his collaborators claim that 'the primary medical responsibility must be to do the best for the infant, the parents and the family, even if those interests conflict with those of society'.[26] At the same time they indicate that the infants' 'best interests' may in some cases require the recognition that there is no effective treatment and that treatment should be discontinued since it serves no purpose. In other words, compassionate care may require that no further active treatment be given to the infant. In making this decision, although the authors do not advert to this consideration, the physicians and parents must consider the likely future 'quality of life' of the newborn and not merely quantitative years gained. This is a contentious area since some people, and even some physicians, believe that everything that is medically possible, even heroic measures, must be provided for newborns regardless of their prospective quality of life. If this ethical view were adopted it would be very difficult to establish priorities about the allocation of health-care resources in this area since, in principle at least, there would be no limits to the use of such resources. On the other hand no one appears to be prepared to claim that care for disabled newborns is actually, or ought to be, determined solely by cost considerations.[27]

Once again, we are confronted with a situation where a complex set of values are in play: the 'sanctity of human life', the special 'symbolic' position of defenceless and vulnerable infants, the best interests of the child, the likely future 'quality of life' of the newborn, the professional responsibilities of the physicians and other health carers, the comparative costs of health treatment. In a sense the remarkable success of the intensive care of newborns has exacerbated the problem in that it is now possible to attempt treatment of extremely low birthweight infants, where the costs are dramatically increased.[28]

Renal transplantation

Renal transplantation is an area where the just and efficient allocation of scarce resources has always been a central consideration since (a) the availability of donor kidneys is severely restricted relative to the demands of patients suffering from renal failure, and (b) the medical criteria for the use of renal transplants in respect of individual patients are extremely complex.[29]

The process of allocating donor kidneys to particular patients involves a number of different levels of decision-making. There is, first, the personal doctor–patient level, where a doctor and patient decide whether a renal transplant is medically feasible and personally acceptable. Second, there is the institutional level, where physicians in their role as program directors have to decide about the amount of medical resources to be committed to a renal program as against other programs in the institution. Third, there is the state and national level, where the allocation of health-care resources to renal programs has to compete with wider health priorities and even with non-health priorities. Inevitably political considerations play a large part at this level. Fourth, there is the international level, where issues related to the relative needs of developed countries and underdeveloped countries, and of the obligation of the former to allocate some medical and health-care resources to the latter, have to be taken into account.

It might be mentioned here that this latter is an aspect of the health resources allocation debate that has not so far been taken into serious account in Australia, though it has been given some consideration in Europe.[30] The World Health Organisation's call in 1988[31] to set the goal of acceptable levels of health for all peoples, and to diminish the gross inequalities in health-care resources as between developed and developing countries, has not received much notice in Australian or US discussions about health-care resource allocation. What proportion of health funds should be set aside to meet obligations to developing countries is not usually factored into the cost–benefit calculations of health economists.

A recent study makes the point that since 'medical need transcends national boundaries' any account of health care as a universal human right 'should recognise that the greater needs of the poorest countries ought to be met first, before even thinking about improving our own quite tolerable condition'.[32] Unfortunately, in the present climate of economic rationalism, this seems no more than a pious hope. Nevertheless, it is a primary ethical consideration in any allocation of health-care resources.

The decisions made at these different levels may not always harmonise with each other. For example, a decision that a physician may make about allocating a kidney to an individual who is his or her patient may conflict with a decision that the same physician may have to make as director of a renal transplant program in an institution. 'In Australia', it has been said, 'the physician–patient relationship is all important and is the main gate-way by which persons are assessed as suitable to be placed on an allocation list'.[33] If this is so then it places severe restrictions on any attempt to allocate resources in a systematic way at the institutional and national levels. However, as noted before, it has been claimed that physicians can no longer evade the larger social consequences of their decisions and that in recommending a renal transplant in a particular case they must also explicitly take into account both institutional and national resources. (Implicitly, of course, they already do so because in practice their individual advice and decisions are constrained by the level of health-care resources available at the institutional and national levels.)

Here we have a version of the opposition between an approach to health-care resources allocation which is based on health *needs* (given the needs of renal patients, how can we best meet them within a given expenditure?) and an approach based on *cost–benefit* considerations (given that we have such and such a budget for renal transplant programs, how can we best meet the needs of renal patients?). There may appear to be no real difference between these two approaches, since the level of resources available for renal transplants to a large extent reflects the fact that the needs of renal patients are given a certain value or weighting by the community, the medical profession and politicians. Nevertheless, the difference of perspective between the approaches can be important.

The larger question has also been raised: should major bodily organs, because they are so scarce, be considered as individual 'property' or rather as 'assets of the community'? At the first joint meeting of the European Society for Organ Transplantation and the European Renal Association (Munich, 1990) on the theme, *Ethics, Justice and Commerce in Organ Replacement*, the following resolution was proposed: 'Cadaveric organs procured within a community should be considered assets of the community, and the community rather than just the medical profession should determine their allocation through announced criteria'.[34] It is not clear exactly how in practice 'the community' might feasibly determine the allocation of major organs, including kidneys, but it is evident that there is a concern that organs should be allocated according to the principles of justice or fairness. This involves specifying publicly the criteria in accordance with which the allocation of bodily organs is to be effected.

The difficulty, however, is that the medical judgment as to whether a given patient is medically fit or suitable for a renal transplant is very complex, since it depends on immunological compatibility between donor and recipient. Again, it is not always possible to draw a clear line between purely medical indications and non-medical indications such as age or lifestyle. Nevertheless, one can at least distinguish the *obvious* cases of non-medical indications and exclude them as criteria for allocating renal transplants. For example, there now appear to be data to show that the age of the recipient does not adversely affect the

133

outcome of renal transplantation. (Australian figures for 1989 show a 38 per cent increase in the numbers of new patients on renal dialysis who are between the ages of 60 and 79 years.) As it has been put:

> Because there are no guidelines for the application of 'medical fitness' it is very easy for that criterion to be used by physicians to make personal assessments of the person's worth to society. Such a 'social worth' principle would tend to be interpreted adversely to the aged . . . Older persons are often regarded as being economically non-productive, more expensive in the use of health resources and to have had a reasonable 'life innings'. It may also be interpreted adversely to antisocial personality types who may be judged as non-compliers and also to persons with significant criminal convictions.

The same author goes on to argue that 'in programs which are supported by public funds such as exist in Australia, any form of selection on social worth is unacceptable. It is discriminatory, and open to being used capriciously, arbitrarily and unjustly.[35]

However, it might be argued that while this is clear in principle, kidneys and other major organs are in such extremely short supply that in practice some non-medical criteria will inevitably be used to select patients. Some indeed have argued that in a situation of drastic scarcity it is responsible and even just to use such 'social worth' criteria (for example, by not allocating a liver transplant to a chronic alcoholic).

In the celebrated case of the Seattle Artificial Kidney Center at the University of Washington in the early 1970s, the following criteria were used to select patients for dialysis: the patients' emotional maturity and responsibility, their financial resources, their value to the community at large. Using these criteria the selection panel excluded a beatnik on grounds of social value, a woman with a dubious reputation on grounds of lack of responsibility and a logger because of his lack of financial resources. On the other hand, being a scout leader and a Sunday school teacher favoured patients' inclusion in the program.[36]

It might be remarked in parenthesis that considerations of 'social worth' have been suggested in the allocation of reproductive technology resources. The South Australian Reproductive Technology Council has, for example, outlined criteria for prospective IVF parents that are very similar to those used for adoptive parents. It could be argued in this case that 'the best interests of the child' born through the use of that technology justify reference to social worth criteria (for example, whether the couple seeking IVF have been convicted of child abuse). On the other hand, it can also be argued that IVF parents are being assessed and judged, simply because they are infertile, in a way that fertile couples would never tolerate.

There are a number of other factors which have to be taken into account in the allocation of donor kidneys. First, there is a tendency in any health program to favour low risk cases. As it has been put: 'Like all health programs, transplantation programs must be seen to have successful outcomes in order to retain their funding. Unfortunately, if used alone, both this principle and that of "medical efficacy" have the potential to lead to a bias towards selecting the "low cost case" which has the greatest chance of success'.[37] Second, at the clinical level different principles are used in the allocative process: for example, some claim that priority should be given to those in most urgent need, those whose life is imminently threatened; others claim, however, that priority should be given to those who have been waiting in the queue the longest (often because of immunological factors). Third, it has been noted:

> The emphasis placed on tissue matching has a bias against patients who do not have an anglo-saxon background. The most affected group in Australia are Aborigines who are disproportionately represented as a group suffering renal failure in the community and are receiving dialysis treatment, yet only approximately half have transplants, whereas the caucasian statistics show more evenly balanced numbers between transplant and dialysis. The reasons for this disparity include the emphasis which is placed on tissue-matching which means that they will rarely get high tally scores unless an

135

Aboriginal kidney becomes available. Another complication is that
there are cultural reasons as to why such kidney availability is unlikely. Similar arguments would apply to other groupings such as
Asian and European communities.[38]

It is evident from the above that the just or fair allocation of
renal transplants is based upon a complex set of ethical assumptions about (a) whether the donation and reception of a kidney
is a purely personal transaction between donor, physician and
recipient, or whether a kidney is an 'asset of the community'
whose allocation can only be decided by community processes
involving publicly specified criteria; (b) whether medical criteria
alone should be used to determine fitness or suitability for renal
transplants, or whether non-medical ('social worth') criteria
may also be used given the extreme scarcity of kidneys for
transplantation; (c) whether some priority weighting (or 'positive discrimination') should be given to the patients (for
example, Australian Aborigines and other non-Caucasians) disadvantaged by the use of immunological criteria. Unless we are
prepared to make ethical judgments about such issues we cannot
make meaningful decisions about the allocation of health-care
resources in this area.

HIV/AIDS Treatment

Ethical questions relating specifically to health-care resource
allocation issues in the HIV/AIDS area are raised by the large costs
of treatments, educational and preventative programs, research
and so on. (As already remarked, it has been estimated that the
total ongoing treatment costs for an HIV/AIDS sufferer are close
to $934 000: $55 000 in direct health costs, including AZT, and
$879 000 in indirect costs.) This is compounded by the escalat-
ing numbers of HIV/AIDS sufferers.

What proportion of health-care resources should in fairness
be distributed to HIV/AIDS treatment, prevention and control,
mainly (for the moment) directed to one section of the com-

munity, as against other diseases affecting other sections of the community? Again, what proportion of health-care resources should as a matter of justice be allocated to AIDS prevention programs as against the direct treatment and care of AIDS sufferers? These issues are all the more difficult to resolve because of the highly 'political' character of the current HIV/AIDS debate, with diverse interest groups and lobbies — public health groups, health professionals, gay community organisations, 'homophobic' groups of various kinds — all playing an active and vocal role.[39]

Ethical issues also come up apropos of privacy, confidentiality and personal autonomy with regard to the kinds of programs that should be funded. Should AIDS education and prevention programs be restricted to providing people at risk with information on the basis of which they can make their own decisions? Or should they be directed more actively at changing the attitudes of those in the high risk area and at paternalistically restraining their behaviour because of the social effects of HIV/AIDS? Or again, should tests for HIV be made mandatory in certain circumstances (for example, before blood donation or surgical procedures) and should the results of such tests be used to inform others (say, contacts of HIV sufferers) even though this involves a breach of confidentiality? Or would such testing be a gross violation of personal privacy?[40]

One might note here a recent report that 10 000 newborn babies were screened for HIV in New South Wales in Australia in 1989 without parental consent.[41] These tests from ten hospitals were part of a study of the incidence of HIV/AIDS in the community conducted by the National Centre for HIV Epidemiology and Clinical Research and were approved by the respective hospitals' ethics committees on the ground that the public interest outweighed the breach of privacy involved. The New South Wales Privacy Committee, however, severely criticised these tests because parental consent had not been obtained.

There is a tension in Australia between members of the medical profession, who generally favour HIV/AIDS testing, and those (policy makers, lawyers and members of the community) in favour of Commonwealth and state privacy legislation. Thus, in a recent survey of Western Australian physicians — consultant staff members of Perth's major teaching hospitals and fellows of the Royal College of General Practitioners — 74.3 per cent indicated that it was not always necessary to obtain informed consent for HIV testing (general practitioners were markedly more likely to think that consent was necessary than were consultants). The authors of the survey conclude: 'We have shown that the majority opinion of senior members of the medical profession is that specific informed consent should not always be requested, that there is great support for compulsory testing, and that confidentiality may be broken in certain circumstances. The nature of medical practice is to synthesise information and to make judgments which balance many, often competing interests.'[42]

On the other hand, recent privacy and health services legislation strongly emphasises the right to privacy of HIV/AIDS subjects. Thus the Victorian *Health (General Amendment) Act 1988* affirms the right of HIV/AIDS sufferers to keep information of their condition private and confidential, though this right may be overridden in certain special circumstances. There is, however, no statute law to guide medical scientists or practitioners regarding breaches of confidentiality, though there are common law precedents for breaching confidentiality where the lives of other people are at stake.[43]

On a more philosophical level, those who emphasise the value of personal autonomy argue against direct intervention and paternalistic forms of HIV/AIDS education and prevention, which they claim could lead to gross abuses of basic human rights. They argue that sexual activity and sexual lifestyles are essentially private matters and, since HIV/AIDS is mainly transmitted through sexual activity, it should also be seen as being in the private realm. Thus a Canadian bioethicist, Patricia Illingworth, claims that male homosexuals are, through their high risk behaviour, primarily harming themselves. Since it is not the business of the state in a liberal democratic society to prevent people from harming themselves, the state has no right to intervene. It follows from this that 'AIDS education programs which target high risk groups and which go beyond providing them with information about their risks, are paternalistic interferences. From a liberal perspective they are unjustified'.[44] Illingworth makes a similar point in a recent article entitled 'Warning: AIDS health promotion programs may be hazardous to your autonomy'.[45] The same author in her book *AIDS and the Good Society*[46] argues that in the debate about HIV/AIDS public health strategies there has been a conflict between older public health laws relating to epidemic control, where patient privacy was subordinated to what was seen as the good of the community, and newer legislation reflecting more liberal views on the fundamental right to personal privacy. It is no longer sufficient to show merely that HIV/AIDS is an infectious disease in order to claim that it should therefore be subject to state control.

On the other hand, the US bioethicist Ronald Bayer takes the view that contracting and transmitting AIDS cannot be seen as a purely private matter since it has obvious consequences for others. Some degree of state control is therefore legitimate in this sphere. Thus Bayer argues that in some circumstances there is a duty to warn an AIDS sufferer's sexual partners of the former's condition. This duty takes priority over the duty of confidentiality and respect for personal privacy. Again, the behaviour of some HIV-infected individuals who demonstrate utter disregard for the well-being of others is an appropriate subject of state action: 'Consent to sexual intercourse is not consent to exposure to a lethal virus any more than marriage provides a warrant for unconsented sexual intercourse'.[47] Bayer claims that, since the state can intervene in this realm only because of the possibility of harm to others, his position can be reconciled with classical Millian liberalism.

A version of this debate has recently taken place in Australia apropos of suggestions that coercive deterrence is needed to restrain identifiable promiscuous homosexuals or intravenous drug users from infecting Australian Aborigines. No one, it has been argued, is at liberty to engage in sexual behaviour that is likely to spread a fatal disease like AIDS, especially among groups such as Australian Aborigines. Others, however, claim that 'culturally appropriate education', and not the use of coercive means, is the only suitable way of preventing the spread of HIV/AIDS into rural Aboriginal groups. 'It would be paternalism', it has been said, 'and racist to suggest that Aboriginal communities are unable to develop or participate in community education'.[48]

It is clear that any allocation of resources to the HIV/AIDS area must take account of the ethical issues detailed above and that it will make a difference to the mode and extent of resource allocation as to whether the state (a) sees certain high risk behaviour as a purely private matter and takes the attitude that it should restrict itself merely to supplying information to enable homosexuals or intravenous drug users to make their own autonomous decisions about engaging in high-risk HIV/AIDS related behaviour; or (b) plays a paternalistic role in attempting to save people in high risk groups from themselves; or (c) actively intervenes to prevent harm being done to others. One might strike an analogy here with the control of hard drugs on the one hand and cigarette smoking on the other. With regard to the latter, apart from restricting cigarette advertising and smoking in certain places, the state limits itself to supplying information to enable cigarette smokers to make up their own minds; with regard to the former the state has so far taken the attitude that drug use has such grave social consequences that it must be actively prevented and it has been prepared to deploy increasingly large resources in the so-called 'war against drugs'. Those who support active intervention in the HIV/AIDS area see this as analogous to the control of hard drug use. Both are private acts but with grave social consequences.

By way of a general conclusion it is clear that severe constraints are placed upon purely 'rational' cost–benefit approaches to the problem of resource allocation by the ethical assumptions we have been considering. As we have seen, these assumptions bear upon the nature of patient–doctor relationships (for example, patient autonomy vis-à-vis medical paternalism, the physician's obligations to his or her patient vis-à-vis obligations to take a larger social view about resource allocation); the priority to be placed upon certain medical needs and treatments (for example, whether infertility is to be deemed to be a serious human disability or to be merely of 'cosmetic' importance); whether a health-needs based approach should take precedence over a resources cost–benefit approach; whether non-medical ('social worth') criteria are just or unjust and should or should not be used in the apportioning of scarce health resources such as major bodily organs or reproductive technology services to infertile couples; whether bodily organs should be seen as 'assets of the community' in whose allocation the community has a legitimate interest, or whether organ donation should be seen as a private transaction between donors, physicians and recipients; or again whether some form of 'positive discrimination' is justified in the allocation process; whether HIV/AIDS is something that falls within the sphere of private morality or whether it has such potential for harm to others that high risk homosexual or drug user groups should be subject to coercive restriction.

More generally, it is obvious that in many of the issues considered above we are faced with a *prima facie* conflict between ethical values; it is not clear which value should be preferred as against another. It is not clear, for example, that the conduct of HIV/AIDS subjects falls within the sphere of personal morality so that there is no ground for state intervention restricting their behaviour or overriding their claims to privacy. On the other hand, it is equally unclear whether the protection of vulnerable groups in the community (such as the Australian Aborigines) requires the coercive restriction of high risk HIV/AIDS subjects, or even whether such restrictions would be practicable.

141

A further constraint on 'rational' resource allocation comes from the fact that certain health situations have what may be called a powerful 'symbolic' or 'metaphorical' character.[49] Thus intensive care for newborn infants symbolises people's concern for the value of human life and for the protection of the defenceless, so that any attempt to allocate resources in a rational cost–benefit way in this area is seen almost as an attack on the 'sanctity of human life' itself. It is wrong to call these issues 'emotive', but they do set a limit to any kind of rational assessment of health-care priorities, all the more so since politicians and policy makers (and the media) are usually very sensitive to them. Again, they can change in a quite volatile way from time to time; thus, for example, abortion is no longer a symbolic issue for the majority of people in Australia (though it is in the US), whatever they may think about its morality; on the other hand, human embryo experimentation and genetic manipulation in humans certainly is. Again, while most people now accept artificial insemination, they are more hesitant about IVF and surrogacy. IVF still, to some extent, symbolises the medical scientist 'playing God', and surrogacy symbolises an attempt to bring motherhood and reproduction out of the purely 'private' sphere into the 'public' or social sphere. Finally, HIV/AIDS has of course a complex and potent set of symbolic connotations: 'the plague', homophobic fears, disease as divine punishment.

For the most part, utilitarian cost–benefit approaches to health-care resources distribution or allocation neglect the ethical issues we have been considering. Instead, they tend to look at disabilities and diseases and their treatments in a de-contextualised way and establish ranked lists of health-care 'priorities' (duly quantified and costed) as though there were no possibility of real conflict between those priorities.

Reaching community consensus

Granted that the allocation of health-care resources depends upon ethical assumptions or judgments, how do we as a community reach agreement on those assumptions? For example, how do we attain some kind of consensus on how serious a disability infertility is and the proportion of resources that should be apportioned to IVF and other forms of reproductive technologies? As we have seen, some people see infertility as a grave disability which prevents them from having children and forming a family. Given the importance accorded to the family in our society, they ask why the alleviation of infertility should not be accorded much the same importance. Other people, however, see the importance given to having children as the result of socio-cultural factors (pro-natalist attitudes which in turn reflect views about women's identity as women being bound up with fertility and reproduction) and women's 'false consciousness'. For these the allocation of health resources to reproductive technology has a very low priority.

Or again, how do we reach any kind of consensus about the priority to be given to and the allocation of resources for intensive care for low-weight newborn infants, or renal transplant programs, or AIDS programs?

Some have claimed that this is basically a medical matter to be decided by reference to the medical facts about patients and to the professional values of physicians (to preserve life, relieve suffering, maintain health).[50] However, while of course medical data are *relevant* to the allocation of health-care resources they are never *determinative*, precisely because, as we have seen, an evaluative–ethical dimension is always involved in resource allocation. As the philosophers remind us, *values* cannot be derived directly from *facts*. Again, the traditional 'Hippocratic' professional values of physicians are too general and abstract to be of any real use in specific allocative decisions.

For example, medical information about the condition of a renal patient — his or her prognosis with or without treatment, histocompatibility, antibody levels, urgency of treatment — is necessary for deciding whether a patient is a candidate for a renal transplant. But a number of patients may satisfy the purely medical criteria, and in a situation of resource scarcity we need

143

to have a way of deciding between their claims. Again, it has been argued that

> determining what counts as a benefit is inherently controversial and independent of medical facts. One patient may have the greatest chance of survival of acute illness; another may have the greatest predicted years of survival; still another may receive the greatest relief from suffering or morbidity and another may get the most satisfaction. Medical facts alone cannot tell us which of these patients will benefit the most from dialysis or transplant. More critically, even if we knew which patient would benefit the most medically from the procedure, we cannot automatically conclude that that patient should receive the medical procedure. Social utilitarians would insist that we take into account social and other non-medical consequences of assigning the scarce resource — a determination about which physicians surely are not expert.

Others insist that fairness or justice as well as medical or social utility be taken into account in deciding what is an ethical allocation of organs:

> For example, some might argue that justice requires that each candidate receive an equal chance of getting a scarce, social, life-saving resource such as a kidney even if not all have an equal chance of benefiting. They may insist that those who have waited longest or those who are sickest get priority, recognising that these patients may not be the ones who would predictably benefit the most.[51]

Supporters of the market claim that if health-care resource consumers are free to buy resources from entrepreneurial providers, a consensus about health-care priorities will be established quasi-automatically and there will be no need to consult the community directly. Thus in the new reformed Dutch health-care system, consumers and representative consumer organisations are given incentives and information to select cost-effective health insurers who are free to negotiate contracts with providers. The assumption is that if there is market competition among health insurers and in health-care provision, insurers will be forced to select cost-effective providers.[52] This depends, however, on consumers having sufficient expert information to make informed choices about health-care priorities so that they will be able to effect a trade-off between quality of care, treatment and price. Because of this, the Dutch government proposes to support the role of independent consumer organisations to gather and assess information, especially for less-informed demographic subgroups, and to require providers to supply specified data. However, it is not known how or to what extent these consumers will make use of this information.[53]

However, as has been noted before, even if consumers are able to make rational health-care choices and even if the market works to produce the most rational (in cost–benefit terms) allocation of health-resources, it does not follow that that mode of allocation is necessarily the most equitable or just. If we have already determined the broad goals or ends of the health system (for example, the provision of basic health care as a condition of autonomy and the enhancement of equality, justice and patient choice and control) then the means of achieving those goals might very well include some element of market demand and supply. But market forces will not determine the broad goals or ends themselves.

It is often suggested that the community as a whole should be consulted to decide about health expenditure priorities. Indeed, in most discussions of health-care resource allocation this is almost a ritual incantation, it being assumed without question that we all know what 'the community' is and know how to consult it on its wishes and determine what it really wants.

Two forms of community consultation

The most celebrated case of such consultation occurred in the state of Oregon in the US in 1987, when people in the state were asked to decide whether they wanted basic medical services extended to some 3000 disadvantaged people as against continuing a major organ transplant program for some thirty potential patients. Following the decision to help disadvantaged groups and to discontinue the organ transplant program, the Oregon Basic Health Services Act was passed in 1989. Under the Act the Oregon Health Services Commission was set up to determine priorities in health services and to promote community involvement in forming a consensus on the 'social values' to be used to guide allocation decisions.[54] As part of this latter task the commission (which included both providers and consumers) used a 'Quality of Well-being Scale' (QWB) which purports to measure the value that society places on the prevention of death, modes of functional disability, alleviation of pain, depression, visual defects and so on. This was supported by a random-sample telephone survey and by personal surveys. In addition a ranked list of health services was compiled under seventeen categories.

> Some examples of categories include: acute fatal conditions where treatment prevents death, with full recovery to previous health state (e.g. appendicitis); maternity care (e.g. prenatal care, delivery services, post-partum care); preventive care for children (e.g. immunisations, well-child care); acute fatal conditions where treatment prevents death, without full recovery (e.g. stroke); chronic fatal conditions where treatment extends the life span and to some extent improves quality of life (e.g. diabetes).[55]

These categories were put in an order of priority on the basis of information from forty-seven public meetings held throughout Oregon. Within each category specific conditions and/or treatments were given a cost–benefit priority and the resultant basic health services plan was submitted to an independent actuarial firm which determined the cost of delivering each health-care item on the list. The state legislature must consider the commission's order of health-care priorities but it cannot alter them. Its sole task is to determine how many health services can be funded, beginning from the top of the list, and then to decide whether additional funds are necessary to ensure that a basic health services system is provided. Late in 1991 the Oregon state legislature accepted the prioritised list of health services and allocated funds on the basis of the list.[56] However, it now appears that the US government is unwilling to allocate federal funds to the Oregon system.

The Oregon scheme has been seen as a model for basing health-care allocation decisions on community 'grass roots' consultation, and a number of other US states — for example, Vermont, New Jersey and California — appear to be following suit.[57] Community health decisions organisations have emerged in those states and a national American Health Decisions organisation has been founded to co-ordinate the activities of state bodies and to facilitate the creation of new groups.

At the same time there has been some critical reaction to the Oregon scheme, questioning its bias in favour of the health needs of white, middle-class, college-educated members of the community who are able to use 'community consultation' for their own purposes. Again, it has been emphasised that public consultation on health-care resource matters needs to be a continuing process if it is to be effective and that this is an expensive business. Further, it has been pointed out that the health values on which there was consensus among Oregonians are extremely general. Thus, in answer to the question, 'Do Oregonians share a living tradition of values about health care that can help define some package of health services as constituting a common good?', the values given priority were prevention, quality of life, cost-effectiveness, ability to function and equity.[58]

The elaborate Oregon system of community consultation in health-care resource allocation has some affinities with the Quality Adjusted Life Year (QALY) approach, where health conditions and treatments are given a numerical weighting on the basis of objective data and interviews with a representative group of people who estimate the worth or quality of life likely to be brought about by a given treatment. The cost of the treatment is then estimated and the treatment is given a cost–QALY rating. For example, it has been estimated that in the UK it costs $8000 to obtain one QALY through a heart transplant and $1200 for one QALY by hip replacement.

Some have proposed the QALY approach as a sufficient means of resource allocation by itself. Thus, for example, an English health economist has argued that if a medical district had one million pounds growth funding 'its managers would recognise that it could produce 5988 QALYs from advice by general practitioners to stop smoking, 1333 QALYs from hip replacements, and seventy-one QALYs from hospital dialysis. Clearly a health authority wishing to maximise QALYs would invest its one million pounds in advice by general practitioners to stop smoking'.[59]

Critics of the QALY approach have dwelt upon its lack of practicability at the individual patient level, its suspect methodology and its utilitarian philosophical foundations. Thus with regard to selecting cancer patients for treatment priority it has been said:

> Selection involves critical analysis both of use of resources and quality of outcome for the patient. Measuring use of resources is relatively easy, but who measures the quality of the outcome — the clinician or the patient? For example, a treatment which causes partial reduction in the size of a tumour may represent clinical success for the physician but the patient may feel no better for it. On the other hand, patients often declare themselves pleased with a treatment they have received, yet show little evidence of benefit in clinical terms. Quality of outcome is hard to measure. It is therefore difficult to design guidelines which will ensure that scarce or expensive resources are given only to those cancer patients in whom need and likely benefit are greatest.

This observer concludes that while the QALY approach 'may be useful for health planners in choosing between two types of medical procedure, it seems much less appropriate in deciding which patient to treat first when scarce resources are being allocated'.[60]

Other critics have attacked the methods by which weightings are given to certain health conditions and treatments. Thus, it has been claimed that the so-called 'objectivity' of the QALY approach is in fact based upon 'subjective' community views and attitudes determined by highly fallible interview techniques.[61] What a QALY signifies is that, in a structured and usually de-contextualised interview situation, the majority of people (most of whom have no direct experience of the disabilities they are interviewed about) in a particular community at a particular time estimate the relative seriousness of certain disabilities and the effectiveness of certain treatments, in terms of the number of years of 'quality life' they obtain for the patient, as having such and such a numerical equivalent.[62] No doubt it is helpful in any allocative process to know what the majority of people on average *think* are valuable health states and treatments at any one time (in so far as this can be ascertained by consumer choice techniques). But of course we cannot determine ethical values by majority voting in this way. Referring to utilitarian schemes of allocation, Richardson notes that:

> there is ... no consensus on the process by which issues of equity and distribution should be resolved. There is an implication in the literature that such issues should be determined by seeking the opinions of a representative cross-section of the community. Majority voting is not, however, universally accepted as a basis for ethical decision-making in all contexts.[63]

In parenthesis, the difficulties of community consultation for decision-making apropos of health-care resources allocation are shown very clearly in the US National Public Opinion Survey poll commissioned by the Harvard Community Health Care Foundation in 1988. In this survey 1250 people representing a cross-section of the American public were polled, together with 200 physicians, 200 employers, one hundred nurses, one hundred political leaders at the federal and state levels, and fifty labour leaders. Very large differences emerged among the various groups about the criteria to be used and priorities in the allocative process. In particular there was a notable lack of consensus between public views of health needs and the views of health professionals (doctors and nurses). It is fair to assume that if a larger range of views had been canvassed — the old as against the young and middle aged, women as against men, blacks as against whites, other ethnic groups as against whites and blacks — even larger discrepancies would have emerged.[64]

Further evidence of variability in people's judgments about the value or weight to be given to health conditions and treatments is to be found in surveys about preferences related to the age of the patient. Thus a recent survey asked randomly selected members of the public in the UK how they would choose between patients of different ages with the same life-threatening illness. Most respondents chose younger children in preference to older patients, but then found it difficult to discriminate between two-year-old and eight-year-old children and thirty-five-year-old adults and sixty-year-olds.[65]

Because of these difficulties, a number of health economists and planners have adopted a much more modest and cautious attitude to the QALY and other utilitarian approaches to health-care resource allocation. While insisting that these approaches have some value in that they enable us to limit the breadth of disagreement and also the scope of arbitrary decision making, they also admit that the QALY approach is not sufficient to determine such health resource allocation decisions.[66] From a liberal point of view, a more serious flaw in all of these utilitarian schemes is that they they tend to be *dirigiste* in style and to be quite uninterested in patient choice and control of health-care resources. Their supporters often claim that they represent a democratic way of allocating health-care resources in that the preferences of the community are consulted and the list of health-care priorities established on the basis of those preferences. But the preferences of 'the community' are in fact the preferences of the majority (and usually of the most socially powerful, educated and articulate groups), so minority and 'voiceless' groups such as infertile couples, indigenous peoples, and lower-class women, tend to miss out and be marginalised.

Further, once the list of allocation priorities is established, albeit through 'community consultation', the individual patient's choice and capacity for control is severely restricted. A television company which engages in consumer surveys of viewers' preferences and then establishes its program offerings by averaging out those preferences is not being 'democratic' for the simple reason that the viewers have no effective control. The same is true of health-care resource allocation schemes of the Oregon kind.

These various difficulties are, however, secondary to the crucial philosophical objections that can be made against the utilitarian underpinnings of the QALY type approach. In particular, as we have noted, it has been argued that utilitarianism can provide no rationale for *distributing* benefits and costs in an equitable way since it merely examines net aggregate benefits, so that if a large enough number of people receive the benefits, even large harms to a small number will be outweighed by the aggregate benefit to the former.[67] As Amartya Sen has said, the utilitarian is unconcerned with inequalities of utility distribution: 'even the minutest gain in the total utility *sum* would be taken to outweigh distribution inequalities of the most blatant kind'.[68] Again, as we have seen, utilitarianism cannot really give an adequate account of the value of personal autonomy and of its associated values: equality, justice, toleration of ethical diversity. The QALY approach and similar approaches stand or fall on the philosophical validity of utilitarianism as an ethical theory, and if that theory is, as can be shown, philosophically incoherent, those approaches are without any kind of visible support.

We have so far been considering community consultation as a formal and structured process for establishing health-care priorities. However, 'the community' can be understood in a much more diffuse and unstructured way to include all the groups, subgroups, organisations and loose coalitions with some kind of interest in health care. Similarly 'community consultation' can be understood in a much more informal way to mean the very complex interchange and negotiation between those groups, which result eventually in some kind of tentative consensus on health-care priorities. In this informal debate and negotiation, factors of very different kinds play a part: religious and philosophical ideas (for example about the value of human life in its various phases), developments in medical science and technology (for example IVF and the other forms of reproductive and genetic technologies), legal considerations (for example about patient autonomy and the rights of the patient vis-à-vis the physician), changes in professional status (for example the decline of medical paternalism), social developments (for example women's demand for control of their bodies), political and bureaucratic changes (for example the now fashionable demand for 'rational' cost-effective approaches to public utilities in the health, welfare and education area). To some extent we have seen the interplay of such factors in our consideration of the treatment of infertility by the new reproductive technologies, intensive care for low birthweight newborn infants, renal transplant programs and HIV/AIDS programs. It is also instructive to look at the slow and complex development of new ethical and legal attitudes in the community to 'quality of life' considerations and the limitation of medical treatment.[69]

Not all the ethical, legal and social developments that emerge from such a process are *ipso facto* good or desirable (an informal community consultation can be, objectively speaking, just as wrong about ethical values as a formal community consultation) but in an open and pluralistic society there is, perhaps, a greater chance that such developments will be subjected to a more stringent kind of critical purification than is likely in more formally structured and directed approaches like the Oregon scheme.

Many people speak as though we all know what 'the community' is and how to discover what it wants in the realm of health care, very much as Jean-Jacques Rousseau thought we could discover what the 'General Will' was — that is, what the community 'really' wanted. Politicians, for example, are very prone to tell us what 'the community' wants and what it will and will not stand. However, in a liberal society the degree of public agreement or consensus on the ethical issues we have been considering is limited by the very values which are at the heart of such a society. The liberal society is characterised by unconditional respect, as Kant would say, for personal autonomy, and that carries with it a respect for ethical pluralism and a resistance to the state and the law intervening in the realm of personal morality or ethics. That does not imply that the various groups within society should not have their own forms of agreement or consensus about bioethical matters, nor that they should not try to persuade others in the general community. What it does mean is that they cannot expect the state to impose any one of those subgroup consensuses upon the general community.

The limits to planning

Throughout this chapter we have emphasised that the ethical values that are presupposed in any resource allocation scheme set limits to any kind of cost–benefit, utilitarian approach. And the difficulties of reaching consensus on these values impose further limits on so-called 'rational' planning in this domain. Again, even if there is an agreement on basic health values, the possibility of conflict between values is always present. Such conflicts can be irreducible or 'tragic' in the sense that they cannot be resolved by appealing to a higher value. They can, however, often be negotiated, though there are no formal rules or principles for negotiating decisions about resource allocation. From this point of view, the only kind of planning that is available to us is similar to what the political philosopher Karl Popper calls 'piecemeal social engineering'.[70]

Popper distinguishes between social utopianism and the more modest and tentative approach of piecemeal social engineering. The utopian is one who has a clearcut blueprint or rational plan for society and everything is governed by this plan. The attractions of social utopianism are that, apparently, we all know where we stand and we have the (illusory) assurance that we won't be faced by any moral dilemmas or conflicts. Its disadvantages are, as we know all too well, that it often leads to high-minded tyranny by social planners and bureaucrats, and the suppression of the unpredictable diversity of human life. But if we reject utopianism and other forms of 'rational' planning of this kind we are not then faced with anarchy. We can, Popper says, control and improve the social process by concentrating on short-term, flexible and revisable goals. In the sphere of health-care resource allocation we can do a great deal in this way to make the apportionment of scarce resources more just and equitable by looking at, for example, questions of access to various forms of health care, by working out ways (as the consumer movement has done) for individual patients and communities to have greater control over health care, by devising strategies to resist the 'technological imperative' in health care, by being prepared to think small rather than always thinking big.

Above all, in a liberal democratic society we must keep the community debate over health issues open and tolerant so that the various parties to that debate can all contribute to the complex and often lengthy process by which some kind of a liberal consensus on how to approach the basic ethical issues can be achieved. (Intelligent, well-informed and balanced media commentators — extremely rare specimens to date — are essential for this public discussion.) In a liberal democratic society that is the only process — clumsy and fallible as it may often be — that we have at our disposal to reach such a consensus.

NOTES

1. 'Preamble to the constitution of the World Health Organisation', in *World Health Organisation: Basic Documents*, 26th edn, Geneva, who, 1976, p.1.
2. M. Hayry and H. Hayry, 'Health care as a right: fairness and medical resources', *Bioethics*, 4 1990, p.21.
3. J. Richardson, 'Economic assessment of health care: theory and

practice', *Working Paper No. 5*, National Centre for Health Program Evaluation, Canberra, 1990.

4. G. Mooney and U.J. Jensen, 'Changing Values and Changing Policy', in U.J. Jensen and G. Mooney (eds.), *Changing Values in Medical and Health Care Decision Making*, Chichester, John Wiley, 1990, p.187.

5. See, for example, J. Rawls, *A Theory of Justice*, Cambridge, Mass., Harvard University Press, 1971; Bernard Williams, *Ethics and the Limits of Philosophy*, Cambridge, Mass., Harvard University Press, 1985. For criticisms of utilitarianism by philosophers of law, see Joseph Raz, *The Authority of Law*, Oxford, Clarendon Press, 1986, and *The Morality of Freedom*, Oxford, Clarendon Press, 1987; Ronald Dworkin, *Law's Empire*, Cambridge Mass., Harvard University Press, 1986.

6. Joseph Raz, *The Morality of Freedom*, op. cit., pp.417–18.

7. J. Rawls, *A Theory of Justice*, pp.30–1.

8. ibid., p.179.

9. John Stuart Mill, *On Liberty*, R.B. McCallum (ed.), Oxford, Blackwell, 1946, p.9.

10. R.M. Veatch, *A Theory of Medical Ethics*, Basic Books, New York, 1981.

11. H. Mahler, 'Health: A Demystification of Medical Technology', *Lancet*, 1975, pp.829–37.

12. Janice Reid and Peggy Trompf (eds.), *The Health of Aboriginal Australia*, Sydney, Harcourt Brace Jovanovich, 1991. On these issues I am indebted to the paper by Neville Hicks, 'An Approach to Ethical Issues in Public Health', *Proceedings of Australian Bioethics Association Conference*, Melbourne, 1991. See also P.H.N. Wood and E.M. Badely, 'The Origin of Ill-health: An Appraisal of the Strategy for "Health for All" and its Implications', in A. Smith (ed.), *Recent Advances in Community Medicine*, Edinburgh, Churchill Livingstone, 1984, pp.11–37.

13. N. Hicks, ibid., p.83.

14. ibid., pp.84, 85.

15. Stephen Leeder and Jason Grossman, 'Is there more to health than money?', unpublished paper, 1992.

16. S. Tesh, *Hidden arguments: political ideology and disease prevention policy*, New Jersey, Rutgers University Press, 1988, p.34.

17. Daniel Callahan, 'Beyond individualism', *Second Opinion: Health, Faith and Ethics*, 9 1988, p.60.

18. E. Pellegrino, *Humanism and the Physician*, Knoxville, University of Tennessee Press, 1979.

19. See the report by the National Bioethics Consultative Committee, *Access to Reproductive Technology*, Adelaide, 1991.

20. On the relative success of IVF/GIFT — an area which is a 'bioethical minefield of inconsistency and malapplied statistics' — see David Molloy and John Hennessy, 'The regulation of clinical reproductive medicine', in H. Caton (ed.), *Trends in Biomedical Regulation*, Sydney, Butterworths, 1990, pp.191–207.

21. Cited in *Making Health Care Decisions*, Harvard Community Health Plan, Cambridge, Mass., 1988 Annual Report, p.16.

22. The following details are taken from D.I. Tudehope, W. Lee, F. Harris, and C. Addison, 'Cost-analysis of neonatal intensive and special care', *Australian Paediatrics Journal*, 25, 1989, pp.61–5.

23. ibid., p.64.

24. ibid., see also L.J. Murton, L.W. Doyle, W.H. Kitchen, 'Care of very low birthweight infants with limited neonatal intensive care resources', *Medical Journal of Australia*, 146, 1987, pp.78–81.

25. ibid.

26. ibid.

27. Though see Murton *et al.* 'Care of very low birthweight infants with limited neonatal intensive care resources', op. cit.

28. For further discussion of the ethical and legal issues involved in the treatment of disabled newborns, see the contributions by Mr Justice Michael Kirby and Julie Hamblin in *Proceedings of the National Consensus Conference on Neonatal Intensive Care*, Sydney, Department of Health, New South Wales, 1989. See also the contributions by Julie Hamblin and Max Charlesworth in *Proceedings of the Birth Defects Conference*, International Clearinghouse for Birth Defects Monitoring Systems and Australian Teratology Society, Sydney, 1991, and the paper by Loane Skene *The Baby M Inquest: Treating Children with Severe Spina Bifida*, Melbourne, Law Reform Commission of Victoria, 1991. See also Helga Kuhse, 'Quality of life and the death of "Baby M"', *Bioethics*, 6, 1992, pp.233–50. The special problems arising from the donation of organs from newborns, when there are difficulties (as in anencephaly) in determining whether they are 'brain dead', are discussed in a symposium sponsored by the Law Reform Commission of Victoria, the Royal Children's Hospital, Melbourne, and the Australian Association of Paediatrics Centre in March, 1991. See *Anencephalics, Infants and Brain Death: Treatment Options and the Issue of Organ Donation*, Melbourne, Proceedings of Consensus Development Conference, 1992.

29. The following discussion relies to a large extent on the paper by Robyn Layton, 'Allocation of kidneys — community and ethical issues', Ayers Rock Dialysis and Transplant Workshop, 1991. See also R.R.H. Lovell 'Ethics, law and resources at the growing edge of medicine', *Australian and New Zealand Journal of Medicine*, 20, 1990, pp.843-9, on the history of renal treatment in Australia.

30. See, for example, the work of the Centre de Bioéthique at the University of Louvain-la-neuve in Belgium.

31. *From Alma-Ata to the Year 2000*, Geneva, WHO, 1988.

32. M. and H. Hayry, 'Health care as a right', op. cit., p.14; see also Hans Kung, *Global Responsibility*, London, SCM Press, 1991.

33. Layton, 'Allocation of kidneys', op. cit., p.6.

34. Cited in Layton, p.3.

35. Layton, p.7. See also Michael Kirby on the Sage dialysis case in the UK, *Bioethical Decisions and Opportunity Costs*, George Judah Cohen Memorial Lecture, University of Sydney, 1985.

36. See E. Keyserlingk, 'The moral choice: allocation of scarce resources', *Journal of the Canadian Medical Association*, 121, 1979, pp.1388-1406.

37. Layton, 'Allocation of kidneys', op. cit., p.8.

38. ibid., pp.10-11.

39. On the 'political' character of the debate in the US see Ronald Bayer, *Private Acts, Social Consequences*, New York, The Free Press, Macmillan, 1989.

40. See M. Gunderson *et al.*, *AIDS: Testing and Privacy*, Salt Lake City, University of Utah Press, 1989.

41. Annual Report of NSW Privacy Committee, Sydney, 1990.

42. David I. Grave and John B. Mulligan, 'Consent, compulsion and confidentiality in relation to testing for HIV infection: the views of W.A. doctors', *The Medical Journal of Australia*, 152, 1990, pp.174-8.

43. For a perceptive overview, see Margaret J. Lane, 'Privacy Protection and Medical Research — Ethical and Legal Issues in Public Health', *Bioethics News*, Monash Centre for Human Bioethics, 11, 1991, pp.3-12.

44. Patricia Illingworth, 'Bayer Revisited', *Bioethics*, 6, 1992, p.31.

45. In Christine Overall and William Zion (eds.), *Perspectives on AIDS: Ethical and Social Issues*, Toronto, Oxford University Press, 1991.

46. Patricia Illingworth, *AIDS and the Good Society*, London, Routledge, Chapman and Hall, 1991.

47. Ronald Bayer, 'AIDs and liberalism', *Bioethics*, 6, 1992, pp.23-7. See also the same author's *Private Acts, Social Consequences: AIDS and the Politics of Public Health*, op. cit.

48. J. Hyde, 'Why Professor Hollows is Wrong About AIDS', *The Age*, 27 March, 1992.

49. See Susan Sontag, *Illness as a Metaphor*, New York, 1978. Sontag discusses the ways in which cancer and tuberculosis have reflected cultural views of these diseases and those affected by them.

50. See, for example, E. D. Pellegrino and D. C. Thomasma, *For the patient's good: the restoration of beneficence in health care*, New York, Oxford University Press, 1988.

51. R. M. Veatch, 'Who empowers medical doctors to make allocative decisions for dialysis and organ transplantation?', in W. Land and J.B. Dossetor eds., *Organ Replacement Therapy: Ethics, Justice, Commerce*, Berlin, Springer-Verlag, 1991, p.33.

52. Frederik T. Schut, 'Health care reform in the Netherlands: A promising perspective for Australia?', National Health Summit, Sydney, November 1991. See also *Choices in Health Care: A Report by the Government Committee on Choices in Health Care*, The Hague, 1992.

53. ibid., p.19. See also M. Charny *et al.*, 'Britain's new market model of general practice: do consumers know enough to make it work?', *Health Policy*, 14, 1990, pp.243-52, and W. Van der Ven, 'Perestrojka in the Dutch health care system, *European Economic Review*, 35, 1991, pp.430-40.

54. See John Kitzhaber, 'The Oregon experience', in *The Ethics of Allocating Health Resources*, Sydney, NSW Department of Health, 1991, pp.45-55.

55. ibid., p.52.

56. See Paige R. Siper-Metzler, 'Oregon Update', *Hastings Center Report*, Sept./Oct. 1991.

57. See Bruce Jennings, 'Bioethics at the grassroots', *Hastings Center Report*, June/July 1988, and 'Grassroots bioethics revisited: health care priorities and community values', *Hastings Center Report*, Sept./Oct. 1991.

58. A special supplement of the *Hastings Center Report*, May/June 1991, discusses the Oregon scheme. See Charles J. Dougherty, 'Setting Health Priorities: Oregon's Next Step', and David C. Hadorn, 'The Oregon Priority-Setting Exercise: Quality of Life and Public Policy'.

59. A. Maynard, 'Logic in medicine: an economic perspective', *British Medical Journal*, 295, 1987, pp.1537-41. For criticism of Maynard see John Rawles, 'Castigating QALY's', *Journal of Medical Ethics*, 15, 1989, 143-7; 'The QALY Argument', *Journal of Medical Ethics* 16, 1990, pp.93-4.

60. Basil A. Stoll, 'Choosing between cancer patients', *Journal of Medical Ethics*, 16, 1990, p.73.

61. See Hiram Caton,'The Quality Adjusted Life Year: a social technology', *Bioethics Research Notes*, 3, 1991, p.32.
62. On the practical difficulties of measurement and interview techniques in the QALY and other similar approaches see J. Richardson, 'Economic assessment of health care: theory and practice', *The Australian Economic Review*, 1st quarter, 1991, table 2 and table 3.
63. 'Cost utility analysis; what should be measured — utility, value or healthy year equivalents?' *Working Paper* no. 5, Melbourne, Monash University National Centre for Health Program Evaluation, 1990, p.35.
64. Louis Harris and Associates, National Opinion Survey, *Making Difficult Health Care Decisions*, 1988. For a critical overview of the process of community consultation see *Consultation: An Appraisal of Community Perspectives*, Australian Health Ethics Committee, Canberra, 1991.
65. P.A. Lewis and M. Charny, 'Which of two individuals do you treat when only their ages are different and you can't treat both?', *Journal of Medical Ethics*, 15, 1989, pp.28–32.
66. J. Richardson, 'Economic assessment of health care', p.18, and R.J. Verkes and P.J. Thung, 'Medical Decision Analysis', in Jensen and Mooney (eds.), *Changing Values in Medical and Health Care Decision Making*, p.85.
67. R.M. Veatch, *A Theory of Medical Ethics*, New York, Basic Books, 1981.
68. Amartya Sen, 'Equality of what?' in *Liberty, Equality and the Law*, Selected Tanner Lectures on Moral Philosophy, Cambridge, Cambridge University Press, 1987.
69. See, for example, Max Charlesworth, 'What kinds of life are not worth living?', Teratology Conference, Sydney, 1991.
70. *The Open Society and Its Enemies*, 1945, Princeton University Press, 1966, 5th revised edn.

6

Consensus in a Liberal Society

The liberal ideal and bioethical realities

At the end of *The Republic* Plato confesses that the state he has constructed is an ideal, a thought-experiment, and that it would be difficult, even impossible given human self-interest, to realise in practice. Nevertheless as a utopian political regime it has a purpose, Plato suggests, in that it enables us to measure actual political structures and processes against it. Plato's aim, of course, was to show that both tyranny at one extreme and popular or mob democracy at the other could never be just regimes, and that we need the paternalism of an elite group of 'philosopher rulers' to bring about a just society.

To some extent the ideal of the liberal society elaborated here, and its implications for bioethics, plays the same role as Plato's imaginary *polis* in that it enables us to assess the actual state of current bioethical discussion and practice in our society. In many liberal democratic societies the liberal values we have been discussing often exist in a compromised form and there are flagrant inconsistencies in the way those values are applied in bioethical practice. As a result, the respect for personal autonomy, the animating value of the liberal society, is often mixed with various forms of paternalism, both medical and

160

bureaucratic; the state and the law often invade the realm of personal morality and act as moral policemen; the toleration of ethical pluralism is minimised in the name of social unity and cohesion.

In the various bioethical issues we have discussed we have seen these compromises and inconsistencies in operation. Thus, while there have been significant gains in our realisation of the right of people to control the manner of their dying, just as they have a right to control the course of their lives, there is still resistance to admitting that people have, in certain circumstances, a right to bring about their own deaths. Again, while there has been widespread acceptance of new ways of procreation and, to some extent, of a right to 'procreative liberty', there is still much hesitation about certain forms of reproductive technology and such alternative means of family formation as surrogacy arrangements. Finally, in the area of health-care resource allocation or distribution, while there is a concern for justice and the promotion of the values associated with autonomy, the utilitarian cost–benefit approach adopted at present by many health economists and policy makers and bureaucrats — an approach that lends itself to bureaucratic paternalism and *dirigisme* — goes directly counter to these values. There are then still hesitations, backward steps and inconsistencies in the recognition and acceptance of liberal values in the sphere of bioethics, and there remain relics of the older view of things, when the state saw its function as enforcing a basic public morality, whether declared by Rousseau's General Will or by Lord Justice Devlin's 'man on the Clapham omnibus'.

One could mention many other medical ethical and bioethical issues where the gap yawns between the liberal ideal and current ethical discussion and practice. We claim that we are living in a liberal society and yet very often we adopt quite illiberal attitudes in many areas of health ethics, medical ethics and bioethics.

We cannot neglect the political aspect of all this. Many bioethical issues, in particular those arising from the new forms of assisted procreation and those to do with death and dying, are politically sensitive in the sense that lobby groups, including the Churches, bring pressure to bear on their political representatives apropos of these issues. As a result there is a good deal of political wheeling and dealing about them. It often takes considerable courage for a politician to stand up for liberal values in this area: as it has been put, there are no votes in promoting 'dying with dignity' laws or legislation permitting surrogacy arrangements. (What one might call the politics of bioethics is a subject that would repay study.) The role of the media, often exaggerating the sensational aspects of bioethical issues, also does not help the cause of calm and dispassionate community reflection on these questions.

Ethical agreement in a multicultural society

One of the issues briefly discussed in a previous chapter was the idea of a public morality or a community consensus which would be the basis for our judgments in medical ethics in general and bioethics in particular. Many people have claimed that unless we have such a basis of 'core values' bioethical discussion will be futile. This is, no doubt, the hope that many people have of the 'expert' bioethics committees that have proliferated in many countries, as though select groups of quasi-Platonic sages will be able to agree upon and formulate a common bioethical code. Unfortunately, without detracting from the value of such committees, this is a vain hope — they too reflect the ethical pluralism that exists in the community at large. They can, of course, have a valuable educative role in promoting public discussion on bioethical questions, but they cannot realistically be expected to formulate a corpus of ethical principles that would constitute a public or common morality and which would guide the discussion of controversial bioethical issues.[1]

In our discussion of this question it was argued that in a liberal society the only common morality or ethical consensus there could be would be one founded on the primary liberal values —

moral autonomy, autonomy-based equality and justice, and annexed values. In such a society there cannot be any consensus on second-order or 'partisan' or confessional values, for example that heterosexual and monogamous marriage is (as Christians would want to hold) the ethically preferred way of family formation, or that deliberately ending one's life is (as orthodox Jews would want to maintain) against God's will; or that organ transplants violate the integrity of the body and spirit (as Buddhists believe); or, more controversially, that abortion is equivalent to murder of the innocent (as many Christians hold).

These, and many others, are moral positions which various groups in society may legitimately espouse and propagate, but about which we have as a community to agree to disagree. However, once again it is difficult in the hurly-burly of community life, with various sectional or partisan interests being pressed, to maintain this meta-partisan or meta-confessional stance. The difficulty is compounded in a multicultural society where the ethical views of various minority groups are often derived from religious foundations radically different from, and sometimes in conflict with, the quasi-Christian ethics (attenuated and secularised as they may be) of our society.

In France President Mitterrand set up in 1984 a National Consultative Committee on Ethics in the Life and Health Sciences to overview biotechnological and bioethical issues. On that committee, apart from medical and legal and governmental representatives, there are also representatives from what the charter of the committee calls 'the four main philosophical families of France' — Catholicism, Islam (now the second largest religious grouping in France), Protestantism and Marxism. These various groups not only have different ethical views about the issues we have been considering so far; they also have differing views about the foundations of ethics and the nature of the ethical enterprise, as well as about the relationship that ought to obtain between the sphere of ethics or morality on the one hand and that of the law on the other. Many Muslims, for example, believe that if a practice is contrary to Islamic religious law then the state has the right, through the civil law, to prohibit that practice. In fact, in many traditional, religiously based societies the strict distinction that is made in liberal societies between the sphere of morality and that of the law simply does not obtain.

The Salman Rushdie affair is, of course, a dramatic example of the severe and apparently intractable religio-ethical problems that can arise in a multicultural society. Leaving aside the attitudes of those Muslims outside the United Kingdom, many British Muslims also see Rushdie's book as blasphemously and sacrilegiously offensive to their Islamic religious beliefs and at the same time demand that the British law directly intervene in a sphere which, in the majority British culture, is not the state's or the law's concern. Some British Muslims have indeed demanded, in effect, that the British legal system adopt the same view of sacrilege (at least with respect to Islam) as the Islamic *Sharia* or religious law does itself. Here the conflict is not just about differing ethical views, but about the whole nature of ethics and its social implications.

Such cases raise questions about religiously based minority groups, with religiously based ethical and social ideas, within a multicultural society such as Australia. The more general question also arises as to whether the whole idea of multiculturalism is itself an essentially secular one. Thus it might be argued that religious pluralism and tolerance are possible only in a society based upon the secularist premise that the sphere of religion and the sphere of the state are distinct and separate, and further that no religion can make absolutist and exclusivist claims to be the only 'true' or divinely ordained religion. Historically, it might be said, the separation of religion and the state only became possible in Europe with Christianity's loss of power and the collapse of the European religiously confessional societies after the French Revolution. In this view, religious pluralism and multiculturalism presuppose that religious groups give up any absolutist and exclusivist claims and are prepared not merely to tolerate passively other religious and non-religious groups, but to positively respect and welcome them in a genuinely multi-cultural situation. Put in another way, it might be argued that there is a contradiction between multiculturalism (based on liberal values) and absolutist and exclusivist religions.

It is true that the liberal society is based upon a polycentric view of culture — a society composed of a number of quite distinct subcultures, each with its own distinctive set of values. For Mill, indeed, the liberal society is of its very essence pluricultural in this sense. It not only tolerates a wide diversity of experiments in living: it positively welcomes and encourages such diversity as a condition of social and cultural vitality. In fact, the liberal ideal provides the only real basis for a genuinely multicultural society and it is not surprising that most of the attacks on multiculturalism have come from those who are critical of the liberal ideal and who sigh for some kind of 'confessional' and authoritarian society based upon a unitary socio-moral consensus.

If we understand multiculturalism in this way there are a number of implications for religiously based subcultural groups within a liberal society. First, such groups must recognise in some way the value of what we have called cultural polycentrism, as against the monocultural view that a society must have a unitary set of ethical values and framework of meaning, and a unitary cultural consensus. Put in a negative way, if any of the constituent subcultures were to say in effect: we can only live in social relationships with other groups if the values of *our* particular subculture are adopted as the basis of a unitary cultural consensus — then, by definition, a multicultural society is not possible.

As noted before, this raises difficulties for certain religiously based subcultures, that is subcultures where the social consensus is based upon a religious consensus and where citizenship and religious membership are seen as identical. In a liberal society what these religious subcultures have to accept is that they cannot carry over their theocratic or confessional views about the relationship between religion and society into the wider society.

165

Traditional Australian Aboriginal groups find no difficulty in admitting that other non-Aboriginal groups may have their own 'Dreamings' and their own religious Law. Again, some forms of traditional Hinduism admit, on theological grounds, the possibility of different religious 'ways' and of different religio-cultural forms. Certain historical manifestations of Judaism, Christianity and Islam, however, have insisted that their religio–ethical-social values are universal, absolute and exclusive, and that the best that other groups, with competing worldviews and values, can expect is passive toleration. Contemporary forms of Christianity, on the other hand, willingly and positively recognise a degree of relativity both with respect to the various bodies or 'churches' within Christianity and also with respect to the other world-religions. In this view the concept of 'the Church' has undergone a radical transformation from a monocultural or unitary one to what might be called a 'multicultural' or polycentric one. In one sense, indeed, the ecumenical movement within Christianity, and between Christianity and other religions, is a form of ecclesial multiculturalism motivated not just by what is seen to be the unfortunate and regrettable fact of religious division, but also by an awareness that there may be some positive kind of divine meaning in the fact of religious diversity both within and without Christianity.

Multiculturalism also requires that the constituent subgroups recognise some form of the liberal ideal and subscribe to the liberal act of faith that it is possible to have a society without consensus upon a substantive set of moral, religious and social values, save for consensus upon the values of personal autonomy and liberty, with all that they connote. This latter 'consensus' excludes any attempt to impose a particular consensus based upon a partisan or sectional set of moral and social values. In the West the Christian Churches have gradually, if reluctantly, come to terms with the liberal society, although there are spasmodic attempts by some Christian groups to impose their set of religio-ethical values as the social consensus for all, particularly in the area of reproductive and family issues.

(The Vatican *Instruction on Respect for Human Life*, 1987, on reproductive technology, for example, called on the civil authorities to prohibit *in vitro* fertilisation.) Ultra-orthodox forms of Judaism and Islam, however, totally reject the separation between religion and the state and the idea that the state, and the law, can be religiously agnostic. For them the liberal ideal and the multicultural society can, at best, only be tolerated *faute de mieux* and no kind of consensus is possible with those who are in effect 'moral strangers'.[2] Since, as we have seen, many bioethical issues touch upon religio-cultural sensitivities, it is important to work out the relationship of the various subcultural groups in a multicultural society to the values of the liberal society. In essence, as has been said, the various groups may quite legitimately espouse and propagate their own specific religio-moral positions, but at the same time they cannot demand that they be imposed upon the whole community. They must agree to disagree.

Conclusion

From one point of view, the liberal society can appear too abstract and 'thin' an ideal to evoke deep and passionate commitment of the kind that partisan or confessional or sectional positions inspire. It is difficult to get excited, so to speak, about Dworkin's characterisation of the liberal society as one 'whose constitutive morality provides that human beings must be treated as equals by their government'.[3] This is, at first blush, not the kind of ideal that one might be prepared to die for.

The liberal ideal can appear like this because autonomy and its associated values are often seen in negative or weak libertarian terms, as though they simply meant that one could do as one chooses, and as though they were wedded to some kind of atomic and self-interested individualism. But when we see autonomy and its attendant values in a more positive light — one thinks here of Kant, Newman and Mill — the liberal society appears as a richer and more compelling ideal. For Kant the autonomous moral agent or human person is deserving of unconditional respect and there is no more valuable thing in the world than a human person exercising the freedom to choose and follow out her or his own destiny. For Newman the human person 'has a depth within him unfathomable, an infinite abyss of existence'. For Mill the individual is sovereign 'over himself, over his own body and mind'. A society of autonomous, self-determining, moral agents or persons is subject to many risks and dangers, as well as being open to the possibility of degenerating into a narrow and sterile individualism preoccupied with 'rights'. But the liberal act of faith is that such a society is infinitely preferable to a society of moral 'infants' who live under 'authorities', always do what is 'objectively' right and live out their allotted roles in 'traditional' structures, but never really choose their lives for themselves. As Isaiah Berlin has said: the liberal ideal may be possible only in special and rare socio- cultural circumstances and it may be difficult to maintain. But it is, nevertheless, an ideal which represents a major and precious development in humankind's moral consciousness and we should not be deterred by the currently fashionable relativistic views about Western values from acknowledging and honouring it.

NOTES

1. For an interesting philosophical discussion on the possibility of a 'common morality' in a pluralistic society see the recent book by the noted US bioethicist H. Tristram Engelhardt, *Bioethics and Secular Humanism: The Search for a Common Morality*, London, SCM Press, 1991.
2. The term is that of H.T. Engelhardt, ibid.
3. Ronald Dworkin, *Law's Empire*, Cambridge, Mass., Harvard University Press, 1986, p.441.

Index

Dawson, Karen, 100
Devlin, Patrick, 23, 161
donor insemination, 77
Dodds, Susan, 94–5
Dworkin, Ronald, 4, 5, 167
'dying with dignity', 31, 36–8
dying, **ch. 3**
  and the hospital, 55–60
  Hindu attitudes to, 43–4
  Islamic attitudes to, 42–3
  Japanese attitudes to, 44
  Jewish attitudes to, 42–3
  multicultural attitudes to, 41–5

ecumenical movement, 166
embryo experimentation, 100–1
ethical relativism, 18
euthanasia, 6, 33
  and the Nazis, 53
  in the Netherlands, 39–41

family formation, 7, 63–9, 75–7
'false consciousness', 92–3, 125,
feminist views
  on reproductive technologies, 8,
    88–102
  'pro choice' principle, 71, 80–1, 88–9
  'third wave' views, 96–102
Feminist International Network of
  Resistance to Reproductive and
  Genetic Engineering (FINRRAGE),
  79, 93, 97
Firestone, Shulamith, 91
Foot, Philippa, 37–8
Foucault, Michel, 57
freedom of expression, 13–14

Gaze, Beth, 100
gender selection, 101
Gilligan, Carol, 89

hard drugs, 140
health care, 117–18
  right to, 108–9
health-care resources, 8
  distribution of, **ch. 5**
    ethical aspects of, 110–11
    international aspects of, 131–2
    market-based distribution, 110,
      144–5
    problem of, 107–11

public health aspects of, 118–19
'symbolic' aspects of, 142
to disabled newborn infants,
  127–31
to HIV/AIDS treatment, 136–42
to infertility treatment, 125–7
to renal transplantation, 131–6
utilitarian approaches to, 111–17
Hicks, Neville, 118–19
Himmelweit, Susan, 97, 100
Hinduism, 166–7
HIV/AIDS, 136–42
  and personal privacy, 137–40
  costs of treatment, 136
hospital, the, 55–60
human life
  beginning, **ch. 4**
  ending, 6, **ch. 3**
  see also quality of life

Ikemoto, Lisa C., 65, 99
Illingworth, Patricia, 138–9
infertility, 66, 67, 101–2, 123–4
Instruction on Respect for Human Life, 70,
  76, 167
in vitro fertilisation, 63–4, 75–6, 95–6,
  101, 124–6, 128
individualism, 6, 21, 34, 167–8
interests of the child, 70–1, 82–3, 84,
  130, 135
Islam, 163–4, 166–7

Job, 50
Jones, Karen, 94–5
Judaism, 42–3, 166
justice, 115–16, 144–5

Kant, Immanuel, 12–13, 78–9, 167–8
  on suicide, 22–3
killing and 'letting die', 34, 35

laissez faire, 5
liberal society, **ch. 2**, 15–27
  and Christians, 4, 166
  and consensus, 160–8
  and ethical relativism, 4
  and Hinduism, 166
  and Islam, 163–4, 166
  and John Stuart Mill, 15–20
  and multiculturalism, 165
  and procreative freedom, 66–9, 102–3
  and the right to die, 52–5